Using I.T. in Primary School History

Lez Smart

CASSELL

Cassell

Wellington House
125 Strand
London WC2R 0BB

215 Park Avenue South
New York
NY 10003

© Lez Smart 1996

British Library Cataloguing-in-Publication Data
A catalogue record for this book is available from the British Library.

Library of Congress Cataloging-in-Publication Data

Smart, Lez.
    Using I.T. in primary school history / Lez Smart.
        p.   cm. — (Children, teachers, and learning)
    Includes bibliographical references and index.
    ISBN 0–304–32827–8. — ISBN 0–304–32829–4 (pbk.)
    1. History — Great Britain — Computer-assisted instruction.
    2. Great Britain — History — Study and teaching (Elementary)
    I. Title.   II. Series.

    LB1582.G7S53   1995
    372.89'0285–dc20   95–33982
                                                                  CIP

ISBN 0–304–32827–8 (hardback)
        0–304–32829–4 (paperback)

Typeset by Mayhew Typesetting, Rhayader, Powys
Printed and bound in Great Britain by Redwood Books, Trowbridge, Wiltshire

Children, Teachers and Learning Series
General Editor: Cedric Cullingford

Using I.T. in Primary School History

9

Titles in the *Children, Teachers and Learning* Series:

Contents

'In his teaching the wise man guides his students but does not pull them along; he urges them to go forward and does not suppress them; he opens the way but does not take them to the place;

. . . if his students are encouraged to think for themselves we may call the man a good teacher.'

Confucius (*ca* 500 BC)

Series Editor's Foreword

The books in this series stem from the conviction that all those who are concerned with education should have a deep interest in the nature of children's learning. Teaching and policy decisions ultimately depend on an understanding of individual personalities accumulated through experience, observation and research. Too often in recent years decisions on the management of education have had little to do with the realities of children's lives, and too often the interest shown in the performance of teachers, or in the content of the curriculum, has not been balanced by an interest in how children respond to either. The books in this series are based on the conviction that children are not fundamentally different from adults, and that we understand ourselves better by our insight into the nature of children.

The books are designed to appeal to *all* those who are interested in education and who take it as axiomatic that anyone concerned with human nature, culture or the future of civilization is interested in education – in the individual process of learning, as well as what can be done to help it. While each book draws on recent findings in research and is aware of the latest developments in policy, each is written in a style that is clear, readable and free from the jargon that has undermined much scholarly writing, especially in such a relatively new field of study.

Although the audience to be addressed includes all those concerned with education, the most important section of the audience is made up of professional teachers, the teachers who continue to learn and grow and who need both support and stimulation. Teachers are very busy people, whose energies are taken up in coping with difficult circumstances. They deserve material that is stimulating, useful and free of jargon and that is in tune with the practical realities of classrooms.

Each book is based on the principle that the study of education is a discipline in its own right. There was a time when the study of the principles of learning and the individual's response to his or her environment was a collection of parts of other disciplines – history, philosophy, linguistics, sociology and psychology. That time is assumed to be over and the books address those who are interested in the study of children and how they respond to their environment.

Each book is written both to enlighten the readers and to offer practical help to develop their understanding. They therefore not only contain accounts of what we understand about children, but also illuminate these accounts by a series of examples, based on observation of practice. These examples are designed not as a series of rigid steps to be followed, but to show the realities on which the insights are based.

Most people, even educational researchers, agree that research on children's learning has been most disappointing, even when it has not been completely missing. Apart from the general lack of a 'scholarly' educational tradition, the inadequacies of such study come about because of the fear of approaching such a complex area as children's inner lives. Instead of answering curiosity with observation, much educational research has attempted to reduce the problem to simplistic solutions, by isolating a particular hypothesis and trying to improve it, or by trying to focus on what is easy and 'empirical'. These books try to clarify the real complexities of the problem, and are willing to be speculative.

The real disappointment with educational research, however, is that it is rarely read or used. The people most at home with children are often unaware that helpful insights can be offered to them. The study of children and the understanding that comes from self-knowledge are too important to be left to obscurity. In the broad sense real 'research' is carried out by all those engaged in the task of teaching or bringing up children.

All the books share a conviction that the inner worlds of children repay close attention, and that much subsequent behaviour and attitudes depend upon the early years. They also share the conviction that children's natures are not markedly different from those of adults, even if they are more honest about themselves. The process of learning is reviewed as the individual's close and idiosyncratic involvement in events, rather than the passive reception of, and processing of, information.

Cedric Cullingford

Foreword

A decade ago Joanne Francis welcomed the arrival of computers in history classrooms as 'the greatest opportunity since printing for a revolution in teaching and learning' (*Microcomputers and Teaching History*, Longman, 1983, p. 1). Today, information technology (IT) impinges on our daily lives in a myriad ways and society assumes that IT will play an increasing and beneficial part in education and schooling. There is now substantial evidence that IT acts as a powerful motivator within the classroom, and that it can be a useful support for active and collaborative learning. Despite this evidence and a plethora of advantages ascribed to IT, statistical surveys and reviews of the findings of classroom inspectors suggest that IT generally remains under used in schools. Indeed, there is a very considerable disparity between advocacy and implementation with regard to the use of IT in history classrooms.

Although IT has not been at the centre of a revolution in teaching and learning (except perhaps in a few specially created technology schools), there have certainly been major and far-reaching developments in history education in recent years. Politicians and others in many countries have shown a growing interest in the purpose and quality of history in schools, and in standards of pupil attainment. There is now a widespread conviction that pupils studying history should do much more than collect, remember and regurgitate information, though there has been disagreement about the changes necessary to bring this about. It has been increasingly recognized that history teaching which not only passes on historical knowledge but also develops children's understanding of the rules and values of history allows them to understand how and why there are different accounts of the past and the criteria upon which they may be judged. Also there has been much reflection on what it is realistic to expect of children studying history at different ages, how best to plan and provide work appropriate to the abilities of each child, and how best to monitor their progress.

There is an opportunity now not only to build on these recent developments and achievements but also to make further use of IT in history education. As Lez Smart emphasizes in this book, IT in the primary school can be said to be entering 'a second stage of development' in which the challenge is to make better and further use of the educational potential of the new technology in a context of recent achievements that need to be consolidated, rapidly advancing technology and growing awareness of what IT can contribute to teaching and learning.

The distinctive contribution of this book to this 'second stage of development' stems from the author's use of his own classroom experience and research to provide examples of ways in which the use of IT can not only facilitate and enhance children's work on various popular topics in the History National Curriculum but also, simultaneously, advance their IT capability. The pivotal role of the teacher is rightly emphasized throughout and the author provides a rich supply of ideas and examples intended to encourage wider realization of the potential benefits of IT in the primary history classroom. This is done by explaining and then reflecting upon a series of examples which explore the interaction between IT and history in the primary school curriculum. These include a detailed examination of how a database and integrated word-processing package might be used to aid a local study as part of children's work on 'Victorian Britain', how a computer timeline program might usefully contribute to work on 'Life in Tudor Times', and how a CD-ROM might be used to enable children to tackle effectively questions such as 'What kind of homes did the Vikings live in?' and, very importantly, 'How do we know?'

Education should provide children with the best intellectual tools currently available. Recent developments in history education and IT offer the prospect of aiding children's understanding of the concepts, skills and procedures of history. These are indeed powerful tools, more powerful ones than before for making sense of the past and for helping children to understand and cope with the present. This book should prove to be a rich and timely source of ideas and examples for primary school teachers faced with these profound responsibilities and opportunities.

A.K. Dickinson
Department of History, Humanities and Philosophy,
Institute of Education, University of London

For the American Reader

STOP! Before going on, American readers of this valuable book should do four things:

First, imagine Great Britain is located roughly where Michigan is. Distance must not be allowed to obscure the important insights this volume contains.

Second, substitute for the examples taken from British history ('Victorians', 'Vikings' and 'Tudors') our own parallels ('The Gilded Age', 'Spanish Conquistadors' and the 'American Revolution'). Our differing national histories should not distract from the exciting possibilities revealed in these pages.

Third, save for IT (Information Technology), disregard acronyms, commissions and official pronouncements. While the political context for education may vary, the important purposes of teachers on both sides of the Atlantic remain very much the same.

Finally, do not be deterred from reading this book if your students are older than the ones described. The insights to what the very young learner can achieve in the field of history with IT will help us to become more aware of how our own expectations will almost certainly need to be modified in the coming years.

I recommend this book to all involved in the teaching of history. Lez Smart's clarifying observations have relevance for us all, whether we are enthusiastic users of IT in our history teaching or are still considering doing so. It is difficult to imagine that our understanding of just what is possible and how it might be achieved will not be furthered by the reflective analysis contained here.

What is most needed, as the examples reveal, is to instil in students not a sense of contrarian scepticism but rather a positive attitude focused on the search for clarification and refinement, which will lead to a greater understanding. This understanding can only be furthered by helping students to develop the habits of asking 'How do we know?' and 'How do we know this is true?'; of developing their ability to devise ways of finding out; of formulating arguments to support their own hypotheses and identifying what they don't yet know and where they might take their enquiries next. These are the skills of the historian. They are also the basis of education for democracy. The over-reliance on memorization and the atomization of the past which has been foisted on American students by the overuse of multiple-choice examinations in recent years has made little contribution to this much wider and more important agenda. Those who have wondered how to incorporate real critical thinking in classes of pre-teenagers need look no further than the practical examples discussed in this book.

Why this book is so important is that it provides a convincing argument, amply supported by illustrative examples, that the use of IT now enables the youngest learner to be involved in the processes of history in a way that was previously very difficult, if not impossible, to do.

Using a series of examples taken from popular history topics undertaken in British primary schools, the author explores how they have been approached traditionally. He then explains how information technology can be incorporated along with other resources. He illustrates how IT not only *facilitates* what might be being attempted by the teacher but further can *enhance* this by providing opportunities for deeper thinking, better communication of the results, an improved grasp of history itself and sometimes a better understanding on the student's part of the application of these learning skills to other disciplines and life outside school. Most excitingly, however, the author reveals the ways in which IT can bring about learning situations that move the whole process on to a *higher plane*. As he readily acknowledges these are 'big' claims and it will be for each reader to decide if they are supported by the examples used. I certainly found them to be so.

In the process of exploring the above the author outlines and discusses his approach to the teaching of history in the primary years. This includes his application of a 'Key Question' approach ('who', 'what', 'why', 'where', 'when' and 'how do we know') coupled with paired historical concepts – 'similarity and difference', 'continuity and change', and 'cause and effect'. The results produced by such an approach are extraordinary, bearing in mind that some of the children involved are aged 7 and 8 and the oldest is 11.

In the USA Stearns (1993) has recently made the case that the early grades are not too young to start to begin developing historical understanding in a serious way as the basis of later success. And yet one has only to consult recent method books in this area (i.e. Ellis, 1995; Allen and Stevens, 1994) to see how the role and contribution of IT has yet to make any serious impact here. As the author clearly demonstrates, this is a measurable loss for students both immediately and for the future. Becoming historically minded can and should start early in each child's school life. The case studies contained in the following pages offer ideas from which we can all profit; the fact-finding approach, imaginative uses of IT, the seriousness of the purpose all contribute to the positive outcomes reported. No teacher should overlook the impact that the intelligent use of IT can have on what she is seeking to achieve with her students.

Before us lies IT's imagined power. Its potential is truly enormous and has yet to be fully explored. This book makes a contribution to this exploratory process. But IT is not a panacea, nor is it 'plug in and play', where the teacher simply inserts the software and stands back while 'learning' occurs. As the author constantly reminds the reader, the use of IT requires the teacher's active, thoughtful and purposeful participation. He discusses how the teachers in the case-studies drew upon their professional skills to enable the IT to make a real difference to both the learning processes and outcomes for their students.

The author shows a keen awareness of the practicalities of using IT in the classroom in his final chapter, which focuses on 'Classroom considerations'. These 'nuts and bolt' issues – the number of computers, problems of ensuring access, the role of assessment, differences in backgrounds and abilities of the students – can thwart the best of intentions and it is important that these issues are acknowledged and considered. The argument made in the earlier case study chapters is strengthened by this willingness to address these practical yet crucial factors. There is much sound practical advice to be found here for those using or considering using IT in his or her history teaching.

This book attempts to bring theory and practice together in the field of IT in the teaching and learning of history and it succeeds in this aim. It is not a 'tips for teachers' manual although there is much that can, and is likely to, be incorporated into the practice of all who read it. The ever-present reflection on and analysis of the case studies presented make a stimulating contribution to our developing understanding of just how IT can both support, and indeed change, the teaching and learning situation. Such issues are being and will continue to be addressed in classrooms around the world. They make this book of interest and relevance to an international audience.

Dr James B.M. Schick
Department of History, Pittsburg State University, Kansas

References

Allen, M.G. and Stevens, R.L. (1994) *Middle Grade Social Studies: Teaching and Learning for Active and Responsible Citizenship*. Boston: Allyn & Bacon.

Ellis, A.K. (1995) *Teaching and Learning Elementary Social Studies* (5th edn). Boston: Allyn & Bacon.

Stearns, P.N. (1993) *Meaning over Memory: Recasting the Teaching of Culture and History*. Chapel Hill: University of North Carolina Press.

Preface

It was some time in 1983 that I spent a lunch hour in a colleague's classroom listening as he told me all about a 'computer' the school had just been 'given'. This was my first contact with a computer in a school situation. I was most unimpressed! The original BBC 16K machine, with its tape drive and flickery screen, might have made a greater appeal if I been impressed by what it or the 'software' (of course I didn't know it was called that at the time) could do. For me, there seemed much greater potential in the school's other recent acquisition, the video camera. What I was doing, of course, was relating these 'new' things to my existing situation, my class of children, what I had planned for them in the near future and how I could achieve these aims as successfully as possible.

I was certainly in the market for new ideas and new equipment but, as I said to my colleague, 'I don't think this is going to be any use to me.'

Yet only three years later my position had moved so far that I was, with some encouragement, prompted to put pen to paper and write my first-ever article detailing how we had used the computer in a class project on 'Our Weather'. On re-reading this article today, I am slightly embarrassed by its naïvety. At the same time the obvious excitement still leaves a warm feeling. This early attempt to explore in print what I felt at the time, namely, that I had come across a new and powerful tool that could contribute to what I was attempting to do anyway, is something that I am still fascinated by today. I am not sure who used the phrase 'the zeal of the convert' but I suppose I must put my hand up and be counted here.

My interest in IT has never really branched out from the initial criteria I applied at that first meeting – the contribution it could make to the learning situation. I never became interested in how the machinery worked; I still get mixed up when referring to ROM and RAM, am uncertain as to what the different MHz numbers mean and can feel my eyes glaze over when the discussions start to get technical. I am not underestimating the contribution my technical colleagues make, having been reliant on and very grateful for their advice and guidance on numerous occasions – it's just not my agenda.

Alongside my own experience of using IT I have been fortunate to work with a number of very talented teachers, many enthusiastic and imaginative student teachers, and gifted and knowledgeable advisory teachers. I also have been involved in a number of small-scale research projects and publications.

All these are called upon in the following pages as the contribution of IT in the teaching and learning of history in the primary classroom is explored.

However, as all the above people were keenly aware, this interaction between IT and history never occurs in a vacuum. The following pages attempt to explore and reflect upon this interaction in context. That is, within the situation of the primary classroom, with all that implies for the demands and diversity found there. In the mid-1990s, it also means acknowledging the external demands, particularly of the National Curriculum and its assessment requirements.

The second feature which is also found throughout is a recognition of the central role of the individual class teacher in firstly realizing, and then attempting to release, the potential of IT in the primary classroom.

One final common thread will be found in what follows and this is a 'reminder' of the evolutionary development of primary education in England and Wales. To understand the present position of both IT and history one needs to be aware of the developments which have affected it. The National Curriculum is certainly one of these, but only one. Developments in our understanding of how children think and learn and the implications for how we teach and organize the learning environment are probably of greater significance.

What is not attempted in this book is a treatment of *all* aspects of IT or of *all* the possible ways in which it might feature. Rather, the attempt is made to identify *some* of the situations in which IT can make a contribution to popular history topics and to *reflect* upon this contribution. It will be argued that IT in the primary school is entering a second stage of development in the mid-1990s and that reflection upon the initial stage is now appropriate and necessary — nowhere more so than in the teaching of history.

After the numerous innovations and initiatives that primary education was subjected to in the late 1980s and 1990s it is hoped that this slim volume can make a contribution to this reflective process and help to consolidate the progress made.

Acknowledgements

I would like to thank Chris Parker for the contribution he made to the section on IT Capability in Chapter 1. During his years at the National Council for Educational Technology (NCET) Chris was responsible for taking many people's, including my own, understanding of the contribution IT could make to children's educational development a significant step further. This influence continues to be seen in the IT guidance provided for schools to support the Mark II version of the National Curriculum.

I would also like to thank Darryl Taylor, Deputy Headteacher at Albemarle JMI School in Wandsworth, for creating the situation in which the examples of Chapter 3 exploring the use of CD-ROM with children could be undertaken. We both know there is a lot more exploring to be done and analogies with 'tips of icebergs' would seem appropriate here.

I would like to thank Past Forward and ESM for their permission to include the screen shots used in Chapters 3 and 4, respectively.

Thanks are also due to Cassell for patience when the Dearing Review and subsequent rewriting of the National Curriculum meant this project had to be delayed for over a year.

The greatest amount of thanks must, however, be reserved for my family.

To Joseph, Holly and Harry for the interest shown through their teatime questions about 'How many words did you write today, Dad?' and for their understanding as I disappeared into the study on yet another sunny day when the park looked a better and more sensible idea.

To Jenny, for her unrelenting support and encouragement despite the demands the writing of this book made on family life. Many thanks.

CHAPTER 1

History and Information Technology in the Primary School: How We Got to Where We Are

In the mid-1990s it is almost impossible to avoid contact with information technology in the ordinary routines of daily life. Instant debits from bank accounts, electronic library book issue, supermarket barcode readers, quotes for car or home insurance from details given over the phone, theatre, holiday and flight bookings, etc., have become so commonplace that they cease to amaze. Yet only two decades earlier even such a simple and commonplace activity as using a cash dispenser would have been the material of futuristic novels . . .

> She approached the hole in the wall, inserted her small square of plastic, tapped in a number and pressed the arrow pointing at £100. The metal drawer opened silently and the money, all in new crisp notes, slid out. Without checking it she put it into her pocket, collected her plastic square and continued on her way to . . .

At home, Sega and Nintendo consoles, hand-held or plugged into the TV, have become major recreational activities for thousands of children. Computer games and machines have dominated the Christmas Best-selling Toys tables throughout the early 1990s and look likely to continue to do so, although the significant gender imbalance in ownership and time spent on computer games is worth noting for its educational implications.

Just as the computer has become part of the scene in everyday life outside and within the home, this is now the case in the vast majority of the country's primary/middle classrooms (DFE, 1994). The novelty factor has certainly waned even if it has not disappeared totally. (At this stage no comment is made on the use of the technology, simply that it is generally commonplace.)

It is important to remember both the speed and scale of the above developments. It was not until 1984 that every primary school in the country had at least one computer. Even allowing for the fact that many classes still have to share computers, that an increasing percentage of school computers are old and often underpowered, and that there is a tremendous amount of INSET still to be undertaken in this field, there can be no denying that the computer is now an established feature in the primary/middle school.

This, then, is the starting-point for this book, which seeks to make a contribution to the 'second stage of development' of computers in the primary classroom, by suggesting that the challenge is to make better and fuller use of the *educational potential* of this technology. The focus here is on the curriculum area of history, an area the author has been particularly involved in exploring and developing in a wide range of situations, including his own classrooms and with advisory, student and experienced teachers in a range of contexts.

Throughout the late 1980s books written on IT in the curriculum tended to deal with the whole curriculum, with perhaps a chapter on its contribution to each curriculum area (e.g. Senior, 1989; Straker, 1989). The developments in each of the curriculum areas are now such that overview books like these can no longer provide the detailed and reflective treatment required to advance the second stage of development. Books dealing with IT in Science, in Art, in Technology, in PE, each in its own right, are likely to become increasingly common in the second half of the 1990s. This in itself is a comment on how far the use of IT in primary education has come.

The 1980s, the *first* decade of computers in primary schools, saw many different organizations, initiatives, training programmes, orders and guidance, all of which sought to ensure that the computer's potential contribution to the learning situation was developed. There was a very definite sense of haste! A decade later, with the benefit of reflection, it is possible to identify and evaluate some significant features, some culs-de-sac, some mistakes perhaps, some important successes, and maybe even to learn some lessons from these to inform future development.

Approaches to learning and IT

All curriculum decisions, teaching styles and the learning situations thus created reflect a philosophy of education. The fact that some teachers, and in recent years many politicians, have not acknowledged or even realized it, does not change this. This philosophy, implicit or otherwise, has a direct bearing on the way IT is used in the classroom. It is reflected in the way the teacher views her role in the process of learning, her perception of what constitutes knowledge and, most significantly, how children learn. The computer does not, never has, and cannot, sit outside these paradigms. This is not the book in which to embark upon a detailed treatment of these issues, but it is interesting to note the existence of attempts to relate IT to these issues since its introduction in the early 1980s (Garland, 1982; Kelly, 1984; Scrimshaw, 1989; Chandler, 1990). All attempt to place the computer in this wider educational context and to explore the implications for primary school practice as it has *evolved* in the UK. It is now necessary for these issues to be considered by a much wider audience, since the success of developments in stage two will, I suggest, be closely related to the quality of this reflection.

This reflective process will enable primary teachers to acknowledge this dynamic between the assumptions held and its manifestations in practice. An *awareness* of this dynamic interaction, and particularly the fact that it is a two-way process, is a prerequisite for developing effective practice.

The term 'effective practice' rather than the often used 'good practice' has been deliberately chosen because of its neutral connotations. 'Effective practice' is here taken to mean no more than the means and methods employed to best achieve those aims that the school or teacher has set for the children.

The ideas developed and the examples given in this book reflect the author's own philosophy of teaching and learning. So that the reader can, as the Americans say, 'see where I'm coming from', the following paragraph is an attempt to briefly summarize my philosophy.

Education, then, is perceived as something that affects all aspects of the learner as a person. It is far more than merely acquiring certain skills and pockets of knowledge, although the importance of these is not to be minimized in any way. Rather, one has to ensure that this aspect of education is not given undue prominence to the extent that it distorts the overall equation. It is *through* the acquisition of the required knowledge and skills that the personal development which schools claim is also of great importance takes place. It is *through* the child's involvement in the learning process that his or her self-concept develops; the more success that is experienced, the more positive the perception of being a success develops. This feeling of 'self-worth' in the formative years at school is increasingly being identified as an important factor not only in being a success at school but also in how that individual continues to perceive him/herself in later life, with all the wider implications. Personal development certainly includes cognitive development but reaches beyond this to include the development of social skills and of the development of a personal moral code. These aspects are neither contradictory nor exclusive of each other. In a similar way the development of a questioning, independent mind leading to a confident, reflective individual is seen as quite compatible with the development of an awareness, and acceptance of, the responsibilities of membership of a wider society.

From this it can be seen that the *process* of learning itself becomes of the greatest significance. It is through the process itself that all the aspects of being educated come into play together. The learner needs to be actively involved in the process of learning, to be involved in the setting of goals, to perceive the purpose behind what she is asked to do and needs to have the opportunity to take some form of ownership of the task once set. The realization that the 'how we learn' cannot be separated from 'what we learn' is at least as old as the educational writings of the ancient Greeks, with an honourable line of development that runs through Comenius, Locke, Rousseau, Froebel and Dewey. Echoes, faint ones maybe, of this belief can be found in recent DES (1985) and NCC (1993) publications concerned with the overall education of the child rather than merely a particular aspect of it. It is interesting to note that, even in the period of subject/knowledge dominance of the late 1980s and 1990s, the early school inspection frameworks (OFSTED, 1994a) acknowledge this in their criteria for identifying successful schools.

In the following chapters and through the specific examples explored, these fundamental ideas about learning and teaching will be seen to inform the case that is made for the contribution of IT in the primary/middle classroom and specifically within the subject of history.

It will be suggested that the impact of IT in the classroom is much greater than merely being another teaching aid and that IT actually has an effect on the whole learning process. Papert (1980) was one of the most influential, if not the earliest, writers to talk about the potential of the computer to affect dramatically the teaching and learning situation in schools. Reviewing his own ideas just over a decade later (Papert, 1993), he appears disappointed that so little has changed and so many of the opportunities created by the arrival of computers in the classroom seem to have been missed. While sharing some of these feelings I suggest that Papert needs to acknowledge the operating environment he is looking at. Change in education has never been either fast or dramatic and I suggest 'evolution' is probably a more useful and appropriate term when looking at school-based education. Frustrating as this may be at times, it can also be seen as positive in that any sustainable change will have to take account of this to be successful. In Papert's first book (1980) perhaps one of the most important points he made was that the use of IT in schools had the potential to affect the *qualitative* dimension of children's thinking. A decade later one can see this is both accepted and acknowledged in the HMI report on IT in the primary school (DES, 1991a):

> [the dual role of IT] clearly helps existing objectives to be achieved and, more subtly, changes the nature and balance of work within the curriculum. In the future more will be expected of pupils in terms of creative expression, conceptual understanding and high-level thinking because there is less need for routine techniques.

It would be interesting to hear how Papert views the British primary school experience with computers, as all his writings to date refer to American schools.

This HMI quote is nowhere more apparent than in the curriculum area considered in this book. The teaching of history in the primary school has been and will continue to be affected by the arrival of IT. The degree of effect and the direction it takes will, however, be determined by individual schools and the teachers who work there. If this book contributes to the process of helping individual teachers to 'sort out' what it is they are seeking from using IT in their history teaching, and to perhaps suggest ideas and examples for consideration, it will have served its purpose.

Teachers and IT

The author has long held the belief that each individual classroom teacher is the key factor in the take-up and use made of IT in a child's education, and there is an increasing body of research evidence to support this (Heywood and Norman, 1988; Watson, 1993). The potential difficulties of access to hardware, of inappropriate software, of large class sizes, of an over-large and prescriptive curriculum, of over-bureaucratic and time-consuming assessment procedures and more cannot be denied. However, they are more likely to be overcome if the teacher can see a real gain from so doing. Accountants call this the 'cost–benefit factor'.

Further, it is argued that if you know and understand *why* you are doing something, you actually do it better, that is more effectively. Nowhere is this more true than in teaching.

Therefore any consideration about using information technology must ask the 'why' question early in the proceedings. It is suggested that in the haste to prepare teachers to use the new equipment during the mid-1980s this question was not sufficiently addressed. A teacher who might have asked, 'Why should I want to have my children use a computer?' on one of the legendary four-day 'cascade model' training courses of this period would probably have been answered with utilitarian rather than educational reasons.

The children will need to be able to use computers in today's world.

There appears to be no systematic evaluation of the success, or not, of these early training courses with their emphasis on being able to 'handle' the technology, i.e. switch on (or 'power up' as it was introduced to the author), insert a disk (or even tape), boot up, format a disk, save, shut down, etc. Anecdotal evidence and personal experiences suggest that permeation of the ideas and skills shown to the teachers on these courses did not go very deep once they returned to school. However, there is evidence of the success of the later Educational Support Grant (ESG) and Grant for Educational Support and Training (GEST) projects (1988–1994). These grants funded locally based IT advisory teachers and had a very different emphasis, requiring them to work with the teacher within her own classroom and agenda and therefore within her own approach to teaching and learning. HMI (1992) noted that 'The I.T. Advisory Teacher's contribution was particularly effective when they were available to work alongside teachers in their own classrooms.'

Perhaps it was necessary to equip large numbers of teachers with the basic skills in those early days. One just wonders whether, had they also been able to explore how the new equipment could contribute to *what they were seeking to achieve anyway*, they might have been more likely to make use of these basic skills upon their return to school.

It is suggested that the increasing number of teachers who are now putting IT to good use within their classrooms are doing so because they have come to see how it can contribute to the achievement of their wider educational aims, however defined. The management of innovation and the factors that affect the take-up of the new element is a fascinating area in its own right. Here it is interesting to just note two of the necessary factors that are acknowledged (i.e. Rogers and Shoemaker, 1971) to affect the degree of success of an innovation. Firstly, compatibility with the existing aims and values and, secondly, the relative advantage factor in aiding the achievement of these in a more effective way. The important thing that needs to be remembered by all those involved in the development of *successful* IT use in schools is that this will *always be the case* (see Heywood and Norman, 1988) and is not a stage that the profession passed through (Smart, 1995). The (un-witting) application of these and other considerations to the opportunity to use IT as I moved from sceptic to enthusiastic user in my own classroom is documented elsewhere (Smart, 1988).

At the same time some readers will be able to identify and recall comments by teacher colleagues who do not make use of IT:

I don't need a computer to do what I do.

It's not necessary. I can do it better by other means.

and of course they are often right! The 'Three Wise Men' report on primary education in 1992 (DES, 1992) was merely one of the more recent reports/surveys to inform us that the most effective and successful teachers use a mix of methods relating to their short- and long-term aims.

I suggest it is also true for the use of IT in the field of history. The examples and ideas developed in the following chapters seek to show how the systematic and critical use of IT in historical work can enhance and facilitate the studies that would be undertaken anyway and for wider educational reasons. However, it is also suggested that there are times when the use of IT enables things to be done in the classroom that go beyond this 'enhance and facilitate' role, and its use can take the whole learning process on to a different plane that is not achievable by other means. The ideas and examples developed in the following chapters illustrate how the compatibility and relative advantage factors referred to above can operate in a primary/middle classroom. These relate specifically to history, but it will also become apparent that the potential effect on teaching and learning styles could well have an impact beyond this particular discipline.

The final claim, and surprisingly one that appears so obvious it often remains unstated, is that, at the same time as it contributes to the development of the child's knowledge, skills and understanding in history, the use of IT in this context is also making a contribution to the development of that wider IT capability now reflected in the National Curriculum requirements (1995). Throughout this book the claim will be made that this history/IT development is a mutually supportive interaction.

Before moving to more detailed ideas and examples within specific history topics it is necessary to briefly examine the present position of both history and IT in the primary curriculum.

History in the National Curriculum – a good model to build upon

The late 1980s and early 1990s have probably been one of the liveliest and most controversial periods in the teaching of history. Future studies will show how history became *the* most controversial subject in the new National Curriculum. There were bitter debates between professional historians, leading to the formation of new organizations, and long letters in the quality press signed by lists of distinguished professors. There was front-page coverage and lead editorials in the tabloid press and TV feature programmes transmitted during the peak viewing hours. What was to feature in the National Curriculum history document even led to questions during Prime Minister's Question Time in the House of Commons and was duly televised. Indeed, Mrs Thatcher's interest in this component of the curriculum even led one of the 'heavier' Sunday papers to question her constitutional authority in this area in a lead editorial! No other curriculum area made such a stir outside the normal education forums.

The controversy was fundamentally about 'What is history?', 'Why do we teach history?' and 'What history should be taught?' The positions taken in response to these questions would have a direct bearing on 'how' it was believed it should be best taught.

The relevance of this debate and its impact on the resulting Statutory Orders for the issues considered in this book are very significant. However, before considering these further it is necessary to look at this formative 1989/1991 period in a little more depth. By doing so it is possible to see how the resulting Statutory Orders for History came to be shaped in a way that, it is contended here, created real opportunities for the potential of IT to be used in this curriculum area.

The year 1989 was very important for history, especially for the primary school sector. Two significant events occurred. Firstly, HMI published the fourth in its series *Aspects of Primary Education,* which dealt with *The Teaching and Learning of History and Geography* (DES, 1989). Secondly, the Secretary of State for Education set up the History Working Group that was to draw up the proposals for this subject area in the newly created National Curriculum.

The HMI report had a dual task. It had to report on the current state of play in the curriculum areas under consideration and then to identify and provide illustrative details of good practice where HMIs had found it.

The Inspectorate called upon the last major national primary survey conducted in 1978 to provide a baseline for its report on the success of teaching and learning within history and geography. It then compared this with information gathered by inspections up to 1986. With the .publication time lag factor taken into account it was about a decade between the two sets of information.

The language of HMI reports has a tradition of circumspection but this was not the case with this report on history and geography in the primary years and emphasizes the concern the Inspectorate felt.

In 1978 it had found

> Standards of work were generally unsatisfactory . . . the work was judged to be superficial, repetitive and lacking in progression, often involving little more than copying from books. Only in a few classes were children developing an understanding of important concepts and acquiring essential skills (para. 5)

and nearly a decade later:

> The standards of work achieved in history, whether taught separately or as part of topic work, were very disappointing. In the majority of schools history was under-emphasised in the curriculum . . . in infant and lower junior classes teaching about the past was often confined to stories about dinosaurs, cavemen and Romans . . . the over-reliance upon secondary sources enabled children to learn some historical facts but did not foster the development of historical skills. . . . (para. 11)

The report concluded that

> The picture of history and historical aspects of topic work revealed in this illustrative sample of schools (1982–1986) was similar to that found by the national Primary Survey of almost a decade earlier. (para. 26)

This was fairly extreme language from the Inspectorate as they reported on a far from satisfactory situation. However, as was noted above, this was only half of the publication. The second half was concerned with presenting illustrative examples of good practice in the field of history and geography. This was done by identifying the characteristics of successful practice, which were then reinforced by case studies, well illustrated with photographs of children and their work.

Before considering what these characteristics of successful practice consisted of and how they relate to the use of IT, it is necessary to focus on the other significant development for primary history that occurred in 1989: the setting up of the fifth of the National Curriculum Working Groups. It is suggested that the HMI report considered above arrived at a most fortuitous moment and that its impact on the teaching of primary history was much greater than it might have been either two years earlier or later. The terms of reference for the Working Group were to 'advise on the framework for history within the National Curriculum context'. Guidance was given on how this should be approached and it stated that the Working Group should consult

> informally and selectively with relevant interests and (amongst other factors) it should take account of best practice and the results of any relevant research and development. (DES, 1989)

In the further (supplementary) guidance given to the Chairman of the Working Group, the model of history that is envisaged begins to take shape. Content is certainly to the fore but there appear phrases such as

> Overall, they (the programmes of study) should help pupils to acquire and develop an historical approach based on objective analysis of evidence . . .

> . . . the programmes of study should give proper emphasis to the content of historical knowledge and lay the foundation for the progressive development of the processes and skills of historical enquiry. . . . They should assist the progressive acquisition of skills in the collection, objective analysis, interpretation, discriminating use and reporting of evidence from a variety of sources. . . . (DES, 1989)

The model of 'what is history' was quite clearly being laid out. The processes of *what* we know (the knowledge) could not be separated from the *how* we came to know it (the skills). Only by using the two together could any real understanding be developed. Despite the controversy that raged at the time and the subsequent modifications made by the Secretary of State, the Working Group produced a model of history for schools to work to that reflected this balance. Despite subsequent revisions, including the major Dearing Review of 1994 this model has survived intact. Teachers are required to strive for the balanced approach outlined in the Working Group's Final Report. The exposition of what is history and why it should have a place in the primary timetable remains a clear and concise one and is a useful reference point for anyone interested in understanding how the present position arose. As has been suggested, the HMI report on primary history and geography arrived at a most opportune moment, which maximized its impact on the evolving National Curriculum model of history. The case studies detailed in the report, with children actively engaged in the historical process, posing hypotheses, handling and interpreting data, asking questions as they

9

attempted to test their ideas out and all the time constantly adding to their own knowledge base, would also be identified as successful practice within the National Curriculum requirements. As the dust settles (hopefully) on the frantic nature of curriculum change of the early 1990s it is likely that teachers' time and energy will turn from mastering new sets of initials (NCC, SEAC, PCs, SoAs, etc. – all now defunct) to seeking those ideas and frameworks to put their own existing practice alongside as they seek to improve upon it. The model of school history that has evolved since 1990 is a sound one and provides a firm base for future development. Teachers now have a reference point.

It is suggested that the serious deficiencies identified by HMI in the field of primary history since 1978 are much less likely to be found in the next report, whenever that is commissioned. Indeed history in the primary school is probably in a stronger position in the mid-1990s than it has been for many years and it does not seem to be over optimistic to anticipate that progress will continue to be made.

There is no doubt that IT can make a significant contribution to this development, but will it? I believe that it will do so and one of the major aims of this book is to identify and illustrate how this potential has been and can be released. The use of IT in primary history will be shown to have both a supportive and an innovative role to play in the realization of the aims for this curriculum area, as identified within the National Curriculum. The meaningful context that is necessary for the development of the child's IT capability is often provided by history.

However, just as one needs to be aware of the developments, reports, etc. over the last decade to be able to appreciate the present position of primary school history, this is also the case with any attempt to understand the present position of information technology in the primary school. The next section therefore details these developments and explores the way the initial aim of getting children using computers matured into the notion of developing an IT capability for each child. The difference between these two is vast and has profound implications for the use of IT in the primary classroom in this second stage of development that was outlined earlier in the chapter. The significance of these changing perceptions and expectations for the relationship between history and IT in the primary classroom is then explored in the following chapters.

IT in the National Curriculum – from 'using computers' to 'developing an IT capability'

For most primary schools the story began in 1982 when the Department of Trade and Industry extended its Micros in Schools initiative to the primary sector. This scheme was used to fund half the cost of a micro-computer to every primary school. Before this a tiny number of enthusiasts had been using computers in their classrooms but most developments had been in the secondary sector. These developments were largely the result of the work of the Microelectronics Education Programme (MEP), which was set up and funded by the DFE in 1980, and the earlier National Development Programme in Computer Assisted Learning (NDPCAL).

Of course obtaining a computer is merely the first step, as a computer without software is of little use. It is very interesting to see how our views of 'appropriate' software have evolved and changed dramatically since this early period, and this is explored below. To accompany these first microcomputers purchased under the DTI scheme the MEP developed the Micro Primer pack which was issued to all primary schools. Much of the software was content-specific, with the exception of FACTFILE, a database developed for the primary classroom. This piece of software opened up a host of possibilities, and was the first piece of content-free software experienced in most schools. It allowed data collected from first-hand experience and from secondary sources to be entered into the computer, sorted, searched and displayed as graphs and tables. Information about 'ourselves' – height, weight, eye colour, hair colour, etc. – which had always been a popular subject in primary maths and project work, was entered into a database file for the children to explore further. However, some teachers were quick to see how the computer gave greater access to and control over data from other sources – census data, surveys of local shops, categorizing fungi were just some of the examples of the early uses FACTFILE was put to. As will be seen, generic software was gradually to become the mainstay of computer-based activity in the late 1980s and early 1990s and with the emphasis now firmly on 'developing an IT capability' this looks likely to continue. What is changing very rapidly is the sophistication of this generic software, with the advent of CD-ROM/CDI the most obvious manifestation of this to date.

Besides a number, and it must be acknowledged it was a small number, of teachers imposing their own subject or content needs on the software as in the FACTFILE examples above, another early development could be observed. Some teachers took advantage of the opportunities offered by content-free software to tailor it not only to the content being studied, but also to the age, ability and understanding of the child. The contribution of IT in relation to differentiation had been realized by some of these early users (Scrimshaw, 1988) and is still a major area for further development today. Differentiation within the teaching and learning of history in the primary classroom is returned to and explored in greater depth in the final chapter. The alternative, content-based software, is generally more restrictive in the uses it can be put to but was, and in some cases still is, a popular option. Possibly, recent developments in both the power of the computers themselves and the medium used (again CD-ROM and CDI come to the front) may enable such software to become more flexible. The use of generic software demanded a reasonable understanding of the software on the part of the teacher to capitalize on its flexibility. This was especially true in the mid-1980s, but has become rather less so by the mid-1990s. If one accepts the point made earlier that the individual teacher is perhaps the key factor in determining the use made of IT in the primary classroom, this early emphasis on 'safe' software is not really surprising.

The importance of the HMI report on history in the primary school (DES, 1989) has already been considered above, and the parallel report dealing with IT (DES, 1991b) was also a very important one. Like its history and geography counterpart it provided an overview of the existing scene and identified what it felt were important trends and developments before presenting some examples of good practice in this area. With so little other information to draw upon to inform the Working Group who were devising the National Curriculum requirements for this still new element, its 'feed forward' was considerable.

The report noted that by 1990 IT could be seen to be developing under the following headings:

> text handling
> data handling
> adventures and simulations
> logo and control technology

It noted that since the initial introduction of computers the range of available software has mushroomed, much of it being produced by a cottage industry which grew up around the microcomputer into education. Much of this software was variable in quality and a considerable amount focused on content, with drill and skill support for mathematics and English, quiz-style programs and tests to the fore. However, amongst those teachers using computers extensively the report noted the trend referred to above and suggested that a more evaluative approach to software was developing. It was obvious that the criterion being applied by teachers in this process was the benefit, or relative advantage (see above), that it contributed to their teaching and learning agenda and that the generic content-free programs were perceived as having the most to offer. Journals such as the *Journal of Computer Assisted Learning, Educational Computing, British Journal of Educational Technology, Education 3–13* and *Junior Education* from the late 1980s abound with enthusiastic teachers' accounts of how the use of these 'content-free' programs contributed to topics undertaken with their classes in ways that surpassed their initial expectations. The professional subject journals of maths, history, geography and science associations added 'Computer update' sections or devoted whole issues to a consideration of what and how IT might contribute in their own area.

'Benefit' and 'advantage' were key words in much of this literature with the emphasis on enhancing and extending subject understanding. The notion of the development of, or progression in, technological understanding itself was not yet a key part of this agenda. The awareness of the technological dimension and the development of the concept of an IT capability that would be developed through and alongside this facilitating and enhancing role was not long in arriving.

Before considering this further development it is interesting just to identify what were these perceived benefits and advantages. Underwood and Underwood (1990) attempted to identify what seemed to be the most common benefits being claimed for the use of computers in the primary classroom during this period. These included children's enjoyment in their work with computers, the chance for children to work at their own pace, gains made in increased motivation, deeper understandings being developed in different disciplines, improved creativity, improved presentation, the creation of a context for collaborative learning to occur and increased chances of success for children with learning difficulties, to mention the most frequently quoted. Some of these and other benefits are explored in more detail in the following chapters.

It was the early discussions and eventual statutory orders for technology in the new National Curriculum that took the development of IT in schools a very significant step forward.

The thinking to this point had been to view IT in terms of its ability to facilitate, enhance and extend learning in most areas of the curriculum and in the areas of text handling, data handling, logo and, in a limited way, control. Early discussions in the working groups which developed the original IT component of the Technology Order were, allegedly, around five attainment targets. One can only assume that the five attainment targets were subsumed into one as a result of the growing pressure for a reduction in the number of attainment targets in maths and science, which had already been published. These five attainment targets could still be picked out of the resulting single attainment target and of course, reappeared as the five strands in the Non-Statutory Guidance (NSG) issued to schools to support the original order (DES, 1990b).

IT capability

The notion of IT capability which emerged in the Technology Order was a very important development. Whilst still linking IT with other subjects of the

National Curriculum it introduced a body of knowledge, skills and understanding which was distinctive to IT. This capability reflected and brought together the developments of the previous decade and the slow but increasing realization that it was through the use of these generic, open-ended programs that IT would make its major contribution in schools.

These five strands were identified within the Non-statutory Guidance section of the orders as communicating information, handling information, modelling and measurement and control. An additional aspect was added with the fifth strand, entitled 'Application and Effects', which required the children to develop an awareness of how their use of IT related to its use in the wider world beyond school. Together these gave a different perspective on IT in school than the one of merely being a tool. The requirement to develop the strands of IT in all curriculum areas remained, but the IT capability as defined here now required that a much more evaluative approach be developed with the children. True, IT was 'only a fifth of one-tenth of the National Curriculum', appearing as it did in the back of the Technology Orders with their emphasis on design technology, but it now had an attainment target, statements of attainment and programmes of study for each Key Stage. As will be seen, this capability was to be honed further in the Mark II model that was to succeed the original National Curriculum in 1995.

The division of what was required into strands, whilst helpful in the planning and organization of IT, was not totally satisfactory as there was always some overlap between them. A further difficulty and confusion arose because 'applications and effects' was treated as a separate strand rather than as a development of each of the preceding four, which of course it had to be.

While there is no disputing that the status of IT had been raised by its inclusion in the new National Curriculum, the actual use and quality of use within this National Curriculum framework was described as patchy both within and between schools (OFSTED, 1994b). It is likely that few schools covered the full range of activities required in the original version. Support was obviously needed in most schools, and this is where the IT advisory teachers really played a major part in attempting to consolidate and spread the developments of the previous eight to ten years within this new National Curriculum framework (HMI, 1992). The most positive areas of development were those associated with the work of advisory teachers for IT, where their ability to go and work alongside individual teachers in their own classrooms *on topics they would be undertaking anyway* was a key element in their success (HMI, 1992). This 'tuning in to existing agendas' is, it is suggested, the key to successful innovation, as was explored earlier in this chapter. It is also the basis of the following chapters, where all the historical topics considered are ones that would be undertaken anyway, with or without an IT presence. The basis of the success of the initial Information Technology in Schools initiative was to a large extent evidence of this. The decreasing impact the IT advisory teachers had when they were forced, for financial reasons and depleted numbers, to operate at a distance in the post-1990 period (OFSTED, 1994b) was predictable.

The National Curriculum requirements for IT also brought the resource issues sharply into focus. It rapidly became clear that a minimum of one computer per class was necessary if children were to have any chance of developing their IT capability as opposed to using a computer occasionally to extend or enhance a subject activity. Few schools have been in the fortunate position of being able to make long-term plans to acquire adequate equipment and to replace ageing computers. The annual allocation from GEST funds has helped to keep the situation ticking over, but the stage has been reached where the original 1982–84 equipment cannot be repaired and the purchase of new equipment barely keeps pace with the need to replace it. Consequently, it is difficult to move to a position of additional computers in classrooms. The significance of this *vis à vis* other factors in affecting the contribution IT might make in the teaching of primary history is explored in greater depth in the final chapter. Insufficient and often unreliable machines, large class sizes, teachers lacking in IT competence and confidence, and the sheer turmoil and stress caused by the imposition of the new National Curriculum did not provide the most conducive environment to expect great progress to be achieved. The integration of the computer into the general work of the classroom that is *implicit* in the concept of developing an IT capability, as opposed to using it as a mere servicing tool, was also, and remains, a real challenge to much existing practice. The culture of rotas and 'turns', which developed as a response to the requirement in the 1990 statutory orders that children must have some IT experience, appears to have been quite widespread. The problems with this approach are also considered in some depth in the final chapter. What the National Curriculum had done, however, was to show that IT would not go away and that all schools and individual teachers would have to begin to think about the issues of identifying what IT experiences were taking place for the children, in what aspects, in which areas of the curriculum and, of course, how it was being assessed and recorded. Despite some useful publications to support these developments (i.e. NCET, 1991; Parker and Smart, 1992), there is little evidence that any but the tiniest number of schools are doing this successfully. It is identified as one of the major issues to be addressed by the HMI report on IT in Schools (OFSTED, 1994b) and is likely to remain so for several more years yet to come.

The fact that such a scenario has occurred in some schools where an IT policy has been agreed and implemented, plans for the inclusion of IT in topics and themes have been developed, programmes of staff development have been put into place and IT has been given the status and value it

15

demanded as part of the National Curriculum, provides insights as to what can be achieved. In this situation, where the framework for developing IT capability is in place, schools have moved steadily forward. The framework of a policy and scheme of work has proved to be an essential ingredient in successfully providing a broad yet appropriate range of IT experiences for children that attempts to ensure both continuity and progression.

The 'modest progress' phrase used by the Chief HMI in his annual report on the development of IT capability since the introduction of the National Curriculum (OFSTED, 1995) is fair comment and probably as much as could be expected in the turbulent days of the early 1990s.

THE DEARING REVIEW

The reasons for the failure of the original version of the National Curriculum and the setting up of the Dearing Review in 1993 are not within the scope of this present book and can be read about elsewhere. What is of significance here is the impact the review had on IT. The Interim Report (NCC/SEAC, 1993) of the Dearing Review moved the status of IT up several notches, recommending that it be viewed as a core skill alongside literacy and numeracy. It stated that IT 'must be located securely at the heart of the National Curriculum'. However, the final report and the subsequent revised order, for whatever reason, pulled back from this position but did separate IT out from Design and Technology. The 9 areas of the primary National Curriculum Mark I had become 10, as IT was now listed as a foundation subject in its own right. The programme of study for IT now has a tighter structure while the breadth and range of IT experiences required are hardly reduced. Is this a step forward? Is it a case of status enhanced by becoming a foundation subject or one of missed opportunity by failure to be identified as a core skill, as suggested in the Interim Report? It is quite simply too early to comment on as yet but within five years or so answers to these questions should be possible.

There is obviously going to be a considerable amount of settling down in the period following the arrival of the Mark II version of the National Curriculum in September 1995, and the role and location of IT in the whole curriculum are likely to be discussed afresh. However, it is interesting to note that the Framework for Inspection (OFSTED, 1994a) of schools identifies IT as a key skill, as well as a subject in the National Curriculum. The framework requires school inspection reports to outline:

Standards achieved by pupils . . .
their competence in the key skills within reading, writing, speaking and listening, number and information technology, the curriculum as a whole.
(OFSTED, 1994c)

Just where the inspectors will look for evidence of this will be of interest in the immediate post-1995 period. The steady evolution and direction taken by IT in the primary school since the mid-1980s as considered above is unlikely to change. The guidance issued by both SCAA (1995) and NCET (1995) in relation to the new order certainly requires no sudden change of direction. They both draw attention to the section in the new orders where it states:

Pupils should be given the opportunities, where appropriate, to develop and apply their IT capability in their study of National Curriculum subjects.
(IT, PoS; DFE, 1995)

What will be required in more detail than previously is just where this is happening and what is actually being achieved, how it is being assessed and recorded and how this information will contribute to the issues of continuity and progression being tackled more effectively.

As the NCET (1995) guidance states,

It is necessary to identify situations where
- subject and IT capability development take place
- subject development takes place and IT capability is consolidated
- IT capability is developed and subjects are consolidated.

This is an interesting and useful classification, although there will inevitably be some difficulties in identifying where consolidation ends and development begins. The reader is invited to consider this question when reading the chapters involving examples of children working on specific historical topics.

The Revised Order for IT (1995) is reproduced here in full so that the breadth of experience now required can be seen in its entirety. The contribution that different subject areas can make in acting as meaningful contexts is likely to feature prominently when schools re-examine their curriculum plans in response to the National Curriculum Mark II model. The particular contribution of history to this agenda is then explored in the following chapters. What history, or rather the children's development in history, gains from this contribution is the key issue for this present work.

The Orders (DFE, 1995) read:

Pupils should have opportunities to:
1a
use IT to explore and solve problems in the context of work across a variety of subjects;
1b
use IT to further their understanding of information that they have retrieved and processed;

1c

examine and discuss their experiences of IT, and assess its value in their working practices;

1d

investigate parallels with the use of IT in the wider world, consider the effects of such uses, and compare them with other methods.

Pupils should be taught to:

2a

use IT equipment and software to communicate ideas and information in a variety of forms, incorporating text, graphs, pictures and sound, as appropriate, showing sensitivity to the needs of their audience;

2b

use IT equipment and software to organise, reorganise and analyse ideas and information;

2c

select suitable information and media, and classify and prepare information for processing with IT, checking for accuracy;

2d

interpret, analyse and check the plausibility of information held on IT systems, and select the elements required for particular purposes, considering the consequences of any errors;

3a

create, test, modify and store sequences of instructions to control events;

3b

use IT equipment and software to monitor external events;

3c

explore the effects of changing variables in simulations and similar packages, to ask and answer questions of the 'What would happen if . . .? type;

3d

recognise patterns and relationships in the results obtained from IT based models and simulations, predicting the outcomes of different decisions that could be made.

The structure of this new programme of study differs from the old order in that it does not detail the specifics of what has to be taught but outlines in general terms the elements of IT that children must have experience of. It is in many ways a concentrated or distilled version of the old order. To implement this in a systematic way will require schools to build these elements into schemes of work right across the curriculum. Every subject order now contains a parallel statement:

> Pupils should be given opportunities to apply and develop their information technology (IT) capability in their study of this subject, where appropriate. (IT, PoS; DFE, 1995)

The end product, the overall aim in this foundation subject is now to develop the IT capability as defined here:

> Information technology capability is characterised by an ability to use IT tools and information sources effectively to analyse, process and present information and to model, monitor and control external events. (IT, PoS; DFE, 1995)

The progression from one Key Stage to another is clearly outlined with the 'confident and purposeful use of IT' at Key Stage 1 being developed to 'becoming a discerning user' in Key Stage 2.

> Pupils should be taught to extend the range of IT tools that they use for communication, investigation and control; become discerning in their use of IT; select information sources and media for their suitability for purpose; and assess the value of IT in their working practices. (IT, PoS; Key Stage 2; DFE, 1995)

The use of IT in the examples in the following chapters will make a significant contribution to both the development and consolidation of the features listed here. The greater the progress made by each child in relation to the above the more confident and competent and discerning, that is, *more capable*, he/she will become in using IT in his/her studies in history. This in turn will further develop this capability.

The following chapters are therefore based on this model of history as it evolved from the above developments. The model of this subject adopted by the National Curriculum is one that requires each child to be the active participant in her historical studies as opposed to being a passive recipient. Such a model requires each child to be involved in developing the skills of historical enquiry as well as acquiring a strong knowledge base. Developed together, the belief is that children will have a better understanding of the past and of its significance for today.

The following chapters work within this National Curriculum framework and each explores one of the major historical topics that is required to be taught in Key Stage 2. Throughout, the intention is to suggest and illustrate how the use of IT can contribute to the study that would be undertaken anyway. Earlier in this chapter it was seen how the twin development of both the knowledge base *and* the development of the skills of history is considered necessary to lead to a child's understanding in this curriculum area. It is the intention of this book to show how IT can make a major contribution in both of these areas. Each of the chapters follows a similar format.

The historical topic is reviewed in relation to the pre-National Curriculum scene, calling upon any relevant reports, guidelines, etc. (i.e. HMI). The requirements of the National Curriculum relating to this topic are then identified and these become the reference points for the illustrative material that follows.

These take the form of a series of examples where it is intended to show how the use of IT:

(a) facilitates the realization of the objectives for the task undertaken;

and/or

(b) enhances what might have been achieved by creating new possibilities or opening avenues that would not have been possible, or would have been very difficult if IT had not been used;

(c) *on occasions* can take the learning situation on to a higher plane than is achievable by other means.

Although these two aspects of the contribution of IT have been separated here, in effect they often occur simultaneously, as one develops out of the other. This will be clearly seen in the examples given.

However, as has been explored in the previous section, it is not enough to merely identify and illustrate IT's contribution. The actual *realization* of this potential within a classroom is dependent on a wide range of factors, of which the teacher's awareness of the possible benefits is a key one. It will always remain one among many others and the final chapter therefore addresses classroom consideration issues which cannot be sidestepped. These include the management of IT in the classroom, key issues such as differentiation, access and the wider equal opportunities area and also assessment and record-keeping. It is hoped that by addressing some of these wider issues and offering some ideas and suggestions in relation to them they will come to be viewed as difficulties to be overcome rather than problems which prevent progress.

Throughout each example an attempt will be made to identify which aspects of this IT capability might have been developed through the examples considered. Schools will need to map and audit each child's IT experience in a much more systematic way in the coming years to ensure that the experiences of the early years are built upon rather than merely replicated as they move through Key Stages 2 and 3. By attempting to identify which aspects of the IT capability have been worked towards with the children through these topics, it is intended to make a contribution to this process. The issue of how these might be assessed and what might count as evidence is addressed in the final chapter on Classroom Considerations. Attention is drawn to assessment opportunities and potential evidence within the topic chapters as and when they occur.

References

Chandler, D. (1990) The educational ideology of the computer. *British Journal of Educational Technology*, **21**(3), 165–174.

DES (1985) *The Curriculum from 5–16. Curriculum Matters 2*. London: HMSO.

DES (1989) *Aspects of Primary Education: The Teaching and Learning of History and Geography*. London: HMSO.

DES (1990a) *National Curriculum History Working Group – Final Report*. London: DES.

DES (1990b) *Technology in the National Curriculum*. London: HMSO.

DES (1991a) *History in the National Curriculum*. London: HMSO.

DES (1991b) *Aspects of Primary Practice: The Teaching and Learning of Information Technology*. London: HMSO.

DES (1991c) *History Non-statutory Guidance*. London: HMSO.

DES (1992) *Curriculum Organisation and Classroom Practice in Primary Schools: A Discussion Paper*. London: DES.

DFE (1994) *Statistical Bulletin: Survey of IT in Schools*. London: DFE.

DFE (1995) *Key Stages 1 and 2 of the National Curriculum*. London: HMSO.

Garland, R. (ed.) (1982) *Microcomputers and Children in the Primary School*. Sussex: Falmer.

Heywood, G. and Norman, P. (1988) Problems of educational innovation: the primary teacher's response to using the microcomputer. *Journal of Computer Assisted Learning*, **4**, 34–43.

HMI (1992) *The Impact of the Information Technology in Schools Initiative 1988–1990*. London: OFSTED.

Kelly, A.V. (ed.) (1984) *Microcomputers and the Curriculum*. London: Harper & Row.

NCC (1993) *Spiritual and Moral Education: A Discussion Paper*. York: NCC.

NCC/SEAC (1993) *The National Curriculum and Its Assessment: An Interim Report by Sir Ron Dearing*. London: HMSO.

NCET (1991) *Focus on IT*. Coventry: NCET.

NCET (1995) *Approaches to IT Capability*. Coventry: NCET.

OFSTED (1994a) *Framework for Inspection of Schools*. London: OFSTED.

OFSTED (1994b) *Information Technology in Schools: The Impact of the IT in Schools Initiative 1990–1993*. London: OFSTED.

OFSTED (1994c) *Handbook for the Inspection of Schools* (May 1994 Revision). London: OFSTED.

OFSTED (1995) *The Annual Report of Her Majesty's Chief Inspector of Schools 1993/94*. London: OFSTED.

Papert, S. (1980) *Mindstorms: Children, Computers and Powerful Ideas*. Hemel Hempstead, Herts: Harvester Press.

Papert, S. (1993) *The Children's Machine: Rethinking School in the Age of the Computer*. Hemel Hempstead, Herts: Harvester Press.

Parker, C. and Smart, L. (1992) *Making Links*. Coventry: NCET.

Rogers, E. and Shoemaker, F. (1971) *Communication of Innovations: A Cross Cultural Approach*. New York: Free Press.

School Curriculum and Assessment Authority (SCAA) (1995) *Information Technology: The New Requirements*. London: SCAA.

Scrimshaw, P. (1988) Matching tasks to children: can computers help? *Journal of Computer Assisted Learning*, **4**, 71–78.

Scrimshaw, P. (1989) Educational computing: what can philosophy of education contribute? *Journal of Philosophy of Education*, **23**(1), 71–78.

Senior, S. (1989) *Using IT across the National Curriculum*. Sittingbourne: Owlet Books.

Smart, L. (1988) The database as a catalyst. *Journal of Computer Assisted Learning*, **4**(3), 140–149.

Smart, L. (1995) 'Facilitate and enhance', in A. Martin, L. Smart and D. Yeomans (eds), *Information Technology and the Teaching of History: International Perspectives*. Reading: Gordon and Breach.

Straker, A. (1989) *Children Using Computers*. Oxford: Blackwell.

Underwood, J. and Underwood, G. (1990) *Computers and Learning*. Oxford: Blackwell.

Watson, D. (1993) *The Impact Report: An Evaluation of the Impact of Information Technology on Children's Achievements*. London: King's College.

CHAPTER 2

Victorian Britain: A Local Study

The study of the Victorian period has traditionally been a popular choice for a history topic in the primary school. The study of the local area of which the school is a part has similarly been popular (DES, 1989). The National Curriculum Orders (1991 and 1995) for history have acknowledged and affirmed the appropriateness of these choices. Despite the quite drastic pruning in 1994 of the historical periods to be studied (DFE, 1995), both Victorian Britain and local history remain at the heart of the history curriculum for children in Key Stage 2.

There is a strong tradition in English primary education of seeking to base what the children are studying within their own experience, at least as a starting-point. Using the local area creates a learning environment in which there are many opportunities for working outside the classroom, for viewing and handling primary as well as secondary source materials and using the wider community as a source of information: in other words, for *actively involving* the children in their own learning on a topic which helps them to make sense of an aspect of their own world. Pre-National Curriculum work on Victorian Britain would often adopt this approach (DES, 1989) and in effect would be based within the locality. This combination continues to be available within the National Curriculum parameters.

This period and local study combination was identified as one that led to particularly effective learning in history by HMI (DES, 1989) and was presented as an exemplar in its report. This approach received further support in the Non-statutory Guidance (given with the original Orders for History, 1991), where the benefits of such a combination were explored. However, a cautionary note was sounded about preserving the focus of each unit and this would seem an appropriate reminder and should help to ensure that the aims for such a topic remain clear. It should help to prevent local studies being undertaken without relating them to the national scene and, similarly, to prevent the latter being considered almost in the abstract and without any consideration of the local implications.

In the absence of any Non-statutory Guidance (or similar) to support teachers as they respond to the Mark II version of the National Curriculum (1995), the appropriate sections of the original guidance will continue to be of use.

So what is required by the National Curriculum in a historical topic set in Victorian Britain with a particular focus on the locality?

The National Curriculum requirement for the teaching of history at this Key Stage is known as a Programme of Study (PoS) and consists of two parts. The first part is the *Key Elements*, and these are common to all the history topics undertaken. The second part consists of the details given in relation to each topic, whether it be Victorian Britain or the Tudors. Together they are intended to ensure the development of the child's knowledge, skills and understanding of history. At the end of the Key Stage this is assessed in relation to the level descriptions (a somewhat clumsy phrase) of the Attainment Target for this subject (DFE, 1995).

These are produced in full so that the examples which follow can be related to the requirements that each teacher of this curriculum area will be seeking to meet. As was outlined in Chapter 1, the intention is to suggest, illustrate and explore how the use of IT can contribute to the achievement of these aims by a consideration of specific examples.

The National Curriculum history framework therefore consists of two component parts. The first are the Key Elements, which for Key Stage 2 are:

Key Elements

The key elements outlined below are closely related and should be developed through the Study Units, as appropriate. Not all the Key Elements need to be developed in each Study Unit.

Pupils should be taught:

1. **Chronology**
   a. to place the events, people and changes in the periods studied within a chronological framework;
   b. to use dates and terms relating to the passing of time, including ancient, modern, BC, AD, century and decade, and terms that define different periods, *e.g. Tudor, Victorian.*

2. **Range and Depth of Historical Knowledge and Understanding**
   a. about characteristic features of particular periods and societies, including the ideas, beliefs and attitudes of people in the past, and the experiences of men and women; and about the social, cultural, religious and ethnic diversity of the societies studied;
   b. to describe and identify reasons for and results of historical events, situations and changes in the periods studied;
   c. to describe and and make links between the main events, situations and changes both within and across periods.

3. **Interpretations of History**
   a. to identify and give reasons for different ways in which the past is represented and interpreted.

24

4. **Historical Enquiry**

 a. how to find out about aspects of the periods studied, from a range of resources of information, including documents and printed sources, artefacts, pictures and photographs, music, and buildings and sites;

 b. to ask and answer questions, and to select and record information relevant to a topic.

5. **Organisation and Communication**

 a. to recall, select and organise historical information, including dates and terms;

 b. the terms necessary to describe the periods and topics studied, including court, monarch, parliament, nation, civilisations, invasion, conquest, settlement, conversion, slavery, trade, industry, law;

 c. to communicate their knowledge and understanding of history in a variety of ways, including structured narratives and descriptions.

 (National Curriculum History, Key Elements (KS2); DFE, 1995)

These elements are what is required to be taught irrespective of the actual content matter being studied and one can see how the emphasis is placed on the *process* of historical investigation and the communication of the results. This is then complemented by the list of historical periods that are required to be studied. These provide the content matter, the *knowledge* that is to be taught in each Key Stage and for Victorian Britain they consist of:

Study Unit: Victorian Britain

Pupils should be introduced to the lives of men, women and children at different levels of society in Britain and the ways in which they were affected by changes in industry and transport.

Changes in industry and transport

 a. steam power, factories and mass production

 e.g. economic growth and the provision of jobs, for men and women, the impact of mass production on living and working conditions

 b. the growth of railways

 e.g. the work of Robert Stephenson and Isambard Kingdom Brunel, the impact of railways on everyday life

The lives of people at different levels of society in town and country

 c. at work

 e.g. factory life, Lord Shaftsbury and factory reform, Florence Nightingale and nursing, domestic service, agriculture, the armed forces, the merchant marine, workhouses

 d. at home

 e.g. family life, at different levels of society, Victoria and the royal family, the role of religion, public health and medicine

 e. at leisure

 e.g. music, sport, holidays, the Great Exhibition

f. at school

   e.g. Sunday schools, voluntary schools, board schools, public schools

(N.B. The phrases in italics are part of the official Orders but are for example only and are not part of the statutory requirements.)
(History PoS, Key Stage 2; DFE, 1995)

Taken together, it is intended that the *skills* and the *knowledge* will effectively develop that *understanding* that must remain the ultimate aim. This fine balance between knowledge and skills was what the History Working Group sought to maintain through 'The Great History Debate' of the 1989–90 period and the Group deserves more recognition for this achievement than has perhaps been acknowledged to date.

By 1995 the number of units of history to be studied in Key Stage 2 had been reduced but the balance between the historical information to be learned and historical skills to be developed had been maintained – just.

One final ingredient needs to be added to the elements and Victorian unit details listed above before looking at specific examples. As a result of the Dearing Review (NCC/SEAC, 1993b) local history has moved to the heart of the history curriculum for this Key Stage. It is no longer either a supplementary or an extension activity, as it was in the Mark I version, but is now simply another study unit alongside and equal with all the others. Three forms of local study are outlined in this unit, a long-term longitudinal study, the local community's involvement in a particular event, and 'an aspect of the local community which illustrates developments taught in core study units'. It is this last one that is here linked with the study of Victorian Britain.

In the following examples specific aspects of the programme of study (as detailed above) will be focused upon. They will be used to explore how IT can make a contribution to the development of the required historical knowledge, skills and understanding that the teacher would be aiming for with this topic. As was outlined in Chapter 1 the examples will attempt to show that there are times when the appropriate use of IT *facilitates* the realization of these aims. Secondly, in some examples it will be suggested that the use of IT actually *enhances* what might be achieved. No attempt is made to claim that other methods could not produce a similar result, simply that the use of IT leads to it being done more effectively. Finally, as has been suggested, there are occasionally times when the use of IT enables the learning situation to move on to a higher plane and to actually create situations that are not possible, or extremely difficult to achieve by any other means.

'The lives of people . . .'; using census returns

Pupils should be taught about *the lives of* men, women and children at different levels of society. . . . (PoS, History KS2; DFE, 1995)

And of course it is *real* people that is envisaged here, ones who actually lived and not the imaginary/stereotypical ones once presented in primary school history textbooks so widely used in the not-too-distant past. But how does one begin this 'introduction to . . .'?

One of the most important sources of information, for all historians, about the people who lived during this period is the national census, begun in 1801, but of more interest when names and place of origin were added from 1841 onwards. Like all forms of historical evidence it has its deficiencies, but it is an incredibly rich source of information for any historian seeking to explore Victorian society. By the very way it was compiled it focuses on a local area.

The potential use of the information contained within these documents to support historical topics in the primary school has long been acknowledged. However, it will be argued that the arrival of computers in the primary school has meant that the technology is now in place to access this information in a way that was previously very difficult, if not impossible. Use of this important source material prior to this point was problematic; obviously originals could not be used, although photographs of the enumerators' sheets were included in one of the early packs of primary evidence produced for schools, the now almost legendary Jackdaw Series of the early 1970s. There were, however, two basic problems with these. The quality of the photo was rarely good enough to decipher the copperplate handwriting of the enumerator (the person who collated and wrote up all the returns). Secondly, the details on the sheets were almost certainly from an area other than that of the school and therefore failed to make contact with the child's own frame of reference through the locality.

The first technological advance that really allowed the primary school teacher to make use of the census to support his/her studies in history was the photocopier! Now so commonplace it is difficult for many to imagine life without it or to appreciate just how it has facilitated children's access to a range of materials previously beyond contemplation. The census returns are a very good example of this and by the early 1980s it was not uncommon for Teachers' Centres (later to become known as Professional Development Centres) to have bought the complete set of census returns for their area either for schools to borrow or for them to make cheap multiple photocopies of the ones that related to their immediate vicinity. It would, however, be very misleading to suggest that this good practice was widespread (DES, 1985, 1989). Nevertheless the point being made here is that it was possible for primary age children to have access to this important primary evidence.

Elsewhere (Smart, 1992), I explore how I sought to make use of these photocopied census returns in a Victorian/local history topic in the pre-computer years during the mid-1980s. It is shown how it was possible to have pairs of children working on a sheet from the 1871 returns for the street in which the school stood with some degree of success. The flowing hand of many enumerators posed difficulties, but with the aid of magnifying glasses (inadvertently but positively contributing to the image of the historian as detective looking for clues/evidence) a good deal of information could be gleaned and from it, hypotheses posed and answers sought. However, the children's initial enthusiasm for using them waned as they began to struggle with working with an unfamiliar and difficult style of handwriting; they got lost as they moved from one sheet to another seeking to find the data they wanted to answer a question, and became frustrated with the sheer volume of information they were trying to handle. My frustration arose from the fact that I knew the children were capable of posing appropriate questions and hypotheses of the data at their fingertips and also of handling the key concepts, of similarity and difference, of continuity and change, cause and effect, that I was seeking to develop.

It was no more than good fortune that this state of affairs occurred at the same time as computers were beginning to make their presence felt in the primary school. A decade earlier and it is difficult to see how much could have been changed. Yet in the mid-1980s the addition of a computer to this equation made a dramatic difference to what was possible. The use of the word 'addition' is important at this stage for the aims of the history study remained the same. The initial impact of the computer was to facilitate the achievement of these aims and it is this to which attention is now turned. In fact this was to underestimate the contribution the computer could, and did make.

So, in what way did the use of a computer in the classroom make this initial contribution?

Firstly, it made it possible to create a situation whereby the fundamental task of actually reading the information could be circumvented. One could now purchase a range of pre-prepared data files with all the data for a specific locality in a specific year already entered. These could be viewed on screen in a modern font (type style) and the problem of interpreting individual words and letters eliminated. The teacher could now take the class into how the data might be interpreted straight away. The understanding of what a census is and the development of the skills of collation, interpretation, etc., could be advanced.

However, it is within the local history context that the Victorian period is being considered here, and these pre-prepared data files are unlikely to apply to one's own school area. This does not mean they have no contribution to make, for they can be very useful for comparative purposes. However, it is the people who lived in the local street or village or district that form the focus of study here.

Throughout the second half of the 1980s and certainly continuing through into the 1990s there is evidence (Ross, 1983; Knight and Timmins, 1986; Smart, 1988; NCET, 1989; Arkell, 1989; Parker and Smart, 1992) of schools transferring the data from the enumerator's sheets into a data file set up on the school's computer as the first step on the road to facilitating and increasing access to it.

The transfer of this data from the enumerator's sheets to disk and thence to screen is neither impossible nor even very difficult. There was initially some concern about children spending hours entering data into the data file and, rightly, concerns were expressed about whether this time might not be put to a better educational use. However, it is here argued that it is beneficial for children to take ownership of the data they are to work with. The classroom management implications of how this might be undertaken so that children can be involved in entering the necessary amounts of data in a systematic and brief time span are explored in the final chapter. The focus here remains upon the contribution that such material on a computer database can make to the development of children's historical understanding.

The copperplate handwriting of the enumerators is certainly worth admiring and studying on the photocopied sheets. Working in pairs and with the aid of a magnifying glass most children from the middle juniors upwards are capable of having a go at decoding what is on the sheets. The preliminary work undertaken in relation to the concept of a census will of course vary, but an awareness that one column contains occupations and other locations certainly seems to be an advantage, for example, knowing that an atlas can be of use when attempting to work out what that unreadable pair of letters in the middle of the location word is. As I have explored elsewhere (Smart, 1988), however, it is moving beyond this stage that proved to be so difficult and frustrating for both teacher and children. It is suggested that the entry of the data contained on the enumerators' sheets on to a database file on the class/ school computer enables the children to move beyond this first stage.

The census, by definition, gives information about individuals: individual people, individual households and families. Such individual information forms the building blocks of all history, but historians are also interested in the inter-relationships of these individuals, the trends that they may be part of (i.e. movement from country to town), the size of the families, the age at which they went to, and left, school, the occupations they were involved in, etc. When using census material not entered on to a computer database it is far from easy to extrapolate this wider picture. It requires a great deal of labour and this has proved to be a process beyond the capabilities of most primary school children.

For example, an investigation into the ten most common occupations of the women from a hundred entries from the surrounding streets would not be an easy or a quick process. Yet if working from data already entered into the data file, this information could be identified and sorted into categories within minutes by most children. However, it is not the compiling of information that is important in history, but the questions it is used to answer. It is argued that the ability of the computer to do the number crunching for the child actually frees her to think more freely about the questions asked. It actually has a qualitative impact on the level of the child's thinking, as Papert (1980) and later HMI (DES, 1989) identified.

In the topic Our Area in Victorian Times, different groups within a class are working on different aspects of life – work, leisure, school, homes, etc. The guidance given for each group's investigations asks them to identify similarities and differences and continuity and change between life now and life some 120 years ago, the period of the census returns, the intention being to create a situation where the children can begin to ask questions and begin to explore the procedures of history.

As outlined in the Key Elements:

a. how to find out about aspects of the periods studied, from a range of resources of information, including documents and printed sources . . .,

b. to ask and answer questions, and to select and record information relevant to a topic. (History, Key Elements, Key Stage 2; DFE, 1995)

One group, investigating Jobs Now and Jobs Then as its focus for study, sought to compare the types of employment available in the area now and 120 years ago. They found it more difficult to obtain from the sources they had used so far as much information about women as they had on men. They used the census data file to initially browse through the occupations listed. One member of the group noticed the word laundress against a woman whose age was 62. The following account of the conversation is certainly not verbatim. It took place over two days with considerable amounts of time away from the computer consulting other source material, like reference books, local maps, local directories for the area and rewatching a section of the TV series 'How We Used to Live'. It took approximately the following forms:

'What's a laundress?'
'Sounds like laundrette!' Perhaps she ran the laundrette?'
'Did they have laundrettes then?'

'Whose washing was she washing?'
'What address did she live at? Was this one of the rich houses in the area?'
'Were there any other people doing this job?'

'Why was it only women who were laundresses?'
'Why was it only the old women who seemed to have this job?'

'Why did they do it 'cause it's not very nice washing other peoples' clothes?'

'Why did they need the money . . . didn't they get a pension . . .?'

'Perhaps they didn't get pensions so they had to keep working when they got old.'

'Do we still have the same job today?'

'No 'cause they have automatic washing machines in the laundrette now.'

And more.

Having a specific purpose the data file was searched using the available commands to find the incidence of this occupation and to relate it to both sex and age. By combining the information eventually gained with information from other sources, the TV series watched, the interviews with the older residents, the current class reader and the reference books used, the children arrived at the conclusion that older women in their neighbourhood once took in and did other people's washing. This conclusion was substantiated by the evidence collected and is an example of children successfully working in the manner of a historian and making a contribution to the requirements contained in the following Key Elements section.

2. **Range and depth of historical knowledge and understanding**
   a. about characteristic features of particular periods and societies, including the ideas, beliefs and attitudes of people in the past, and the experiences of men and women; and about the social, cultural, religious and ethnic diversity of the societies studied;
   b. to describe and identify reasons for and results of historical events, situations, and changes in the periods studied. (Key Elements KS2; DFE, 1995)

This investigation really did grasp the group's interest and when they eventually reported back on their findings it was the role and contribution of older women both in Victorian times and in the family today that prompted a lively discussion among the whole class.

The above investigations were certainly contributing to the development of historical skills and a deeper understanding but how significant was the IT factor?

THE IT FACTOR − FACILITATING

It is important not to claim too much for any one factor in a learning situation, as there are so many variables in action. Having said this, however, the role of IT would seem to have been an important one, contributing in the following ways.

Firstly, it gave the group easier access to an important historical source of information for the period they were investigating. Of course they *could* have identified the job of laundress from the photocopies and gathered the necessary information to support their hypotheses without the use of a computer. The important question here remains – but *would* they? Would the motivation have remained strong enough? Would it have proved possible to hold the required number of variables in place while seeking extra data to relate to each other, i.e. location, sex and age? Maybe. And there again, maybe not, for there is no doubt that when the children's questions began to require different aspects of the data file to be related to each other, the IT component helped to keep the momentum of the investigation moving.

Secondly, and arising from the above, one of the very early concerns of the OFSTED reports (1993, 1994) into the impact of the National Curriculum on teaching and learning in the primary years was with the incidence of lack of depth in the tasks being undertaken by the children. To move beyond the information given, to be able to move to a situation where one can begin to pose questions/hypotheses of it and therefore to move to any real understanding, in any curriculum area, requires time. Time to reflect upon what you have, to consider ways forward, to explore these, to evaluate the results, or not, obtained – fundamentally to 'get inside' what is being studied. There can be little doubt that this has been one of the casualties of the National Curriculum Mark I model, particularly in the humanities. This was reflected in the responses of teachers to the Dearing Review (NCC/SEAC, 1993a), as they insisted that something must be done about the sheer volume of content prescribed for KS2, which eventually led to the slimming that then took place. However, the pressures on time are unlikely to diminish and the role of IT's contribution here is on a utilitarian level, but is none the less important for that.

Thirdly, by doing the sorting and listing, the number crunching elements, it is argued that it freed the children to continue to ask higher level questions and to pose hypotheses. It enabled the children to move through the task to make it more likely that they would reach this stage where the important, higher level, thinking skills could be employed.

In this aspect one can perhaps begin to see how the facilitating role starts to move into one where the contribution is moving towards an enhancing one.

As has been seen and will be seen throughout this book the contention is that the use of IT in meaningful context is a two-way process. The contribution being made by the above small example to the ongoing development of the children's IT capability can be illustrated by referring to the the first section of the programme of study for IT at this Key Stage.

Pupils should be given opportunities to

a. use IT to explore and solve problems in the context of work across a variety of subjects.
b. use IT to further their understanding of information that they have retrieved or processed.
c. discuss their experiences of using IT and assess its value in their working practices.
d. investigate parallels with the use of IT in the wider world . . . and compare them with other methods. (IT, PoS; DFE, 1995)

The final point of this section is particularly pertinent here, for the holding and manipulating of variables, or more variables than might be otherwise possible, is perhaps one of the most creative uses that IT is put to. The children's developing awareness of how IT can help them do similar things in their school studies is an important part of the IT capability.

THE IT FACTOR — ENHANCING

The previously referred to HMI *Teaching and Learning of IT* (DES, 1991c) makes several points that can be interpreted as examples of where the IT factor contributed in an enhancing way to what the children were engaged in.

In some cases the children's concentration spans were noticeably longer than when they were engaged on conventional work . . . . (para. 35)

. . . extending their (the children's) thinking in ways that would otherwise have been difficult or impossible. (para. 38)

The example detailed above is evidence of these claims made by HMI. Without the use of IT it is most unlikely that the group of children investigating the position of older women in the late Victorian period would have been able to pursue their enquiries as far, or in such depth. The group had no problems with the concepts they were exploring, but they did need *support* with the handling of the sheer amount of information available to them. Once aware of this support they were able to stay with the task and pursue their lines of enquiry. The quality of their observations and conclusions was directly related to the involvement or concentration span that HMI noted (above). The further claim by HMI that IT contributed to the extension of the children's thinking is at the same time both a cause *and* effect of the greater concentration span that the IT factor gave rise to. One can see in the above example how one question about the census data led to another and how these developed into a hypothesis that was then posed.

It is suggested that this is a small-scale example of what Papert talked about in his book, *Mindstorms* (1980). Here he talked about the power of the computer to free up children's thinking, not in a quantitative way but in a qualitative one. Although the interactions between child and computer have not developed quite as Papert (1993) imagined, at least in British primary school classrooms, it continues to inspire. This brilliant and far-seeing book is as relevant today as it was when written, perhaps even more so. Often referred to as ahead of its time in 1980, it is perhaps only now that an increasing number of teachers are becoming aware and confident enough to actually explore the potential of the computer to contribute to this qualitative dimension of children's thinking. This should not really cause a great deal of surprise. In Chapter 1 the central role of the individual teacher in the successful take up and use of IT in the classroom was established. In the light of the upheavals in British primary education during the 1988–1995 period it is at least understandable if a great many teachers were not able to really explore the potential of this innovation. If, however, this interpretation contains an element of accuracy, the second half of the 1990s, which promises to be less unsettled, could be a particularly significant one for IT in the primary classroom.

The use of IT to explore the census material in the above example did much more than merely facilitate access to it. The power of the computer to take the drudgery out of some of the sorting and collating tasks and to give speedy responses actually encouraged the children to speculate further, and to move deeper into their area of study. In effect they were not merely gathering more information about the people they were looking at, but they were also moving closer to a greater understanding of them and their lives. This is when looking at the past really starts to become history!

IT has a further contribution to make in this enhancing role. As was seen above, the key elements for history require that children should be taught

a. how to find out about aspects of the periods studied, from a range of resources of information, including documents and printed sources . . .,

b. to ask and answer questions, and to select and record information relevant to a topic. (History Key Elements KS2; DFE, 1995)

This requirement takes children to the heart of the process of historical enquiry. I think it is *implicit* in these sections of the key elements that the pupils will be involved in making decisions about which sources and resources might be most useful to them as they study a topic. In the proof copies of the new National Curriculum that were sent to every school in November 1994 this section was more precise, with the requirement for 'an understanding of the value of (different) historical sources for the period being studied' being clearly stated. The further pruning that took place between these proofs and the final orders of 1995 saw this sentence disappear, but if the elements are intended to involve children in the processes of historical enquiry, the ability to make informed choices with regard to the value (i.e. usefulness) of available source material must remain part of the agenda. This is not the only time that it has been pointed out that the desire to produce a briefer National Curriculum has had the unfortunate consequence of also leading to a loss of clarity of intentions.

As was seen in the above example, IT certainly facilitated access to the census, but it goes further than this facilitating role. The ability to understand and appreciate the value of a historical source is not an easy one to develop, as it requires comparison of possible alternatives and thus the use of informed judgment. The census is a wonderful source of information on the people who lived in this period and this place but it is, like all sources, a limited one. The incomplete nature of history, the *always* incomplete nature of our knowledge in this field is both a constant fascination and a frustration. This awareness is one that has to be developed with children and of course it needs a context. The children involved in the census work above gradually came to realize just how rich a source it was, but also how it had its limitations. It is suggested that the development of the ability to evaluate the value of (different) historical sources with children is likely to manifest itself in both positive and negative ways.

> 'It's no good trying to use the census for that – let's see if there is anything in the newspaper [p/copy of local newspaper of the 1880s] . . . or that book we've got in the class library.'

was a comment heard when the children were attempting to find out whether old people did get a pension in 1871.

Or the group who were exploring the similarities and differences and continuities and changes between schools and school life across the two periods,

> 'I wonder if the census can tell us when children had to go to school . . . 'cause it's not really an occupation is it? . . .',

after discussion decided to obtain a print out of everyone under 16 along with his/her occupation 'just to see'.

These, it is suggested, are indicative of the small steps that children take as they develop the skills of choosing sources and evaluating their value. No claim is being made that they are developed solely or even chiefly through the use of computer data. However, to make informed choices a wide range is necessary and the IT component here facilitates the access to a very important historical source. Once accessed the increased power and control over this source made possible by the use of IT not only makes the children's searches easier but, it is suggested, positively encourages them to ask more questions, to develop these questions further and to pursue their lines of enquiry more fully and therefore in greater depth. The decreasing incidence of in-depth study (OFSTED, 1993) has already been mentioned and must be treated seriously. Despite the reduction in content in the Mark II model of 1995, it is an area that one hopes OFSTED will continue to monitor. The link between studying something in depth and higher standards is likely to be a close one. The IT component is therefore contributing in a more significant way, as its initial facilitating role becomes a *springboard* for taking children's involvement and thinking about their tasks to new levels. This whole area is returned to in Chapter 5, where it is considered in a broader context than the example considered here.

'The lives of people . . .'; using buildings, making newspapers

The buildings or the remains of buildings of a particular period have always been central to the study of history. They help to give a material context to the lives of the people that are being studied. Why was it built? What is it built of? Who built it? For whom? and Why there? are just some of the many questions that can be asked of any building, whether it be the Parthenon, the Great Wall, the ruins of Masvingo in Zimbabwe, the village lock-up or the clock tower (for example, see Keith, 1991; Purkiss, 1993). The answers arrived at give an insight into what life was like during the period – or more accurately lives, for that of the builder was often likely to be very different from that of the person who ordered the building. These differences are just as likely to be in evidence whether one is considering the building of the Pyramids or the local railway or canal.

It is the process of enquiry that leads to the attempt to answer, or rather to pose informed hypotheses to, the above, and similar questions that take one into the lifestyles of the people involved.

The National Curriculum reflects this importance and lists buildings as one of the named range of resources children should be expected to have experience of:

> how to find out about aspects of the periods studied, from a range of resources of information, including documents and printed sources, artefacts, pictures and photographs, music, and buildings and sites. (History Key Elements KS2; DFE, 1995)

The following explores how this particular requirement can be combined with the one that follows it in this key elements section. This is the one with the subtitle *Organization and Communication* of what the children might have learned, and requires that children should be taught

a. to recall, select and organise historical information, including dates and terms.

b. the terms necessary to describe the periods and topics studied, including court, monarch, parliament, nation, civilisations, invasion, conquest, settlement, conversion, slavery, trade, industry, law.

c. to communicate their knowledge and understanding of history in a variety of ways, including structured narratives and descriptions. (History Key Elements KS2; DFE, 1995)

As with all the other examples used throughout this book the intention is to illustrate and suggest how the appropriate use of IT can make an important contribution and it is argued that this is certainly the case with regard to this section. However, the previous example dealing with the use of the census readily acknowledged that the tasks undertaken had been, and still could, be undertaken without using IT. This is also the case with the two examples considered in this section.

Asking children to make newspapers to demonstrate and present what they have learned about a topic, or an aspect of it, has long been a popular one in the primary years. If anything its use may have increased since the early 1990s as teachers have responded to the English part of the National Curriculum, which requires children to be presented with opportunities to write for different audiences, for different purposes and in different styles:

Pupils should be given opportunities to write for varied purposes . . . They should be taught to use writing as a means of developing, organising and communicating ideas.

Pupils should be taught to write in response to more demanding tasks.

They should be taught to use characteristics of different types of writing. They should be taught to use features of layout and presentation.

Pupils should be encouraged to develop their ability to organise and structure their writing in a variety of ways, using their experience of fiction, poetry and other texts. (National Curriculum English: Writing KS2; DFE, 1995)

The document lists a range of contexts that might provide the basis for this and these include studies in other areas of the curriculum. The use of newspapers/advertisements in history-based topics offers tremendous scope for providing meaningful contexts to tackle the above in. It is, of course, just an example of the holistic nature of the primary curriculum that was explored in Chapter 1.

However, with the focus on the locality during the Victorian period and the development of the children's historical knowledge, skills and understanding through such a study, the use of newspapers and then advertisements is turned to. The contribution that the use of IT can make to this process is explored throughout.

The first example, therefore, explores this form of communicating information in relation to part of this topic on Victorian England/local study, which focused on the built environment.

The second example is closely related to the newspaper format and is that of the advertisement. It will be suggested that involving the children in creating such an advertisement offers something different from the newspaper, although there is no reason why they should not be used together.

Newspapers

Whatever the location, North or South, rural or urban, there is almost certainly a local building that was erected during the Victorian period. This was the era of the municipality and a wide range of buildings arose – town halls, parish rooms, prisons, new parks and cemeteries and of course schools. Many of these indicate the changing economic structure of the Victorian period as reflected in the local area, with new factories and warehouses, new dock complexes, indoor markets and shopping parades being built. Alongside these were the vast numbers of new railway stations with accompanying viaducts and bridges that were also added to the landscape during this period. Then there was the celebratory architecture, some of which touched the above, but would also include clock towers, fountains and large ornamental park gates. These were often erected to commemorate specific events, of which the silver and diamond jubilees of the Queen herself are perhaps the most common. Street names can also be indicative of events and personalities of this period: for example, Jubilee Terrace, Mafeking Street and the Albert Square immortalized by the popular *EastEnders* TV soap opera.

The opening or unveiling of these local buildings and monuments was sometimes part of a national celebration, but were almost always very significant local events in their own right. As such they were usually well reported and documented and many of these records are still in existence, whether as local newspapers, programmes of events or towards the end of the century increasingly as photographs. While the originals are almost certainly held by the local history section of the library service, it is now common to find the local Teachers' or Professional Development Centres holding copies for schools to borrow. A more recent development has seen libraries producing their own copies and collections of photos held in their archives and offering these for sale to the general public as postcards or calendars.

In almost all school locations, therefore, it is likely that the teacher undertaking a topic on the Victorians and with a local emphasis will have at her/his disposal local buildings of the period (all be they in varying states of repair) and accounts, written and/or visual, of their building or opening.

The use to which they are put will vary according to each teacher's aims and the focus for the investigation. These aims will almost certainly include using this information to gain a further insight and understanding of the lives of the people who lived in this area at this time. A key question approach might well be adopted with Why?, When?, Who?, What?, Where? and How? (see Parker and Smart, 1992, for further information on this approach) being used to open up the lines of enquiry with the children. The tasks set up to attempt to answer these questions would probably involve using as wide a range of sources of information as possible and these might include visits to significant (as defined by the teacher's aims for this topic) local buildings and the use of facsimiles of contemporary documentary material. This has long been considered good history and the National Curriculum drew upon this steady evolution in creating its model for schools.

Each teacher will have planned what preparation needs to be undertaken with the children prior to using these materials and making the visits and these plans will almost certainly have included some idea of how the information gained will be used and, at some stage, how the historical understanding that has been developed is communicated. There are many ways of doing this – a book, drama, collage, a class museum to name just a few that can be seen in many primary school classrooms. Alongside these, making a newspaper has been a popular way of asking children to com-municate their new knowledge and understanding. Sugar paper, coloured pencils and felt-tips, scissors and glue have traditionally been used in bringing the children's text and graphics together to this end. This is likely to continue and there is no reason why it shouldn't. Less than a decade ago it replicated what happened every night in the major printing houses located along Fleet Street in London. The desk-top publishing revolution led to this no longer being the case. In schools educational, as opposed to commercial, factors have led/will lead teachers to explore different ways and media for bringing text and graphics together to promote progress in children's development in the fields of history and language. However, if it can be shown that the teacher's aims within these two areas might be facilitated and further enhanced and that a contribution can also be made to the development of the children's IT capability, few would argue that these developments are not worthy of consideration. The following examples and illustrations call upon work that I have been involved in or have seen undertaken in classrooms in the last few years.

Using a newspaper format the class, or different groups within the class, undertook a report on the opening of a significant local building they have been studying. I have seen this take the form of

- a newspaper in the style of the Victorian one with small dense text, few if any photos, appropriate price, etc.
- a newspaper reporting the same event but in a modern style (perhaps emulating the current local newspaper style with banner headlines, lots of photos, interviews, etc.

- a newspaper using both styles on the same page, the old style being used to report on the opening and intended use, etc., the new style being used to report on its current state and using interviews to gather opinions on this.

It is suggested that the use of IT here might make a contribution to the children's historical development in two particular ways.

Firstly, if the children use one of the various desk-top publishing packages now widely found in primary schools they will be able to draft and redraft their reports until they have it exactly as required. For a newspaper, as opposed to a story, this will include taking account of the number of words and the space available and the actual shape (i.e. column or free flow around any graphics) they wish to present their text in. They will also have been able to create the headlines and subheadings in the text size and font they consider most appropriate. All this can, of course be done using felt-tip pens, scissors and glue. As has been noted the scissors and glue approach replicated the way real newspapers were put together until the late 1980s. It was then that the technology developed to a stage where not only the text but also the graphics *and* the layout could be created on a screen and sent direct to the presses. The parallel development in school-based technology means a similar opportunity is now available for children to explore these developments too.

However, the IT component offers something more than just facilitating the processes of newspaper creation. The flexibility offered by the word processing or DTP package will enable the children not just to manipulate what they have written but also enable them to *update* it as new bits of information resulting from research being undertaken on other source material, i.e. photos or personal reminiscences. One of the factors which distinguishes history from other disciplines is the incompleteness of the data that has to be worked with. While it will always be incomplete in relation to any one event, feature or person, there is always the chance that a little more will come to light which will add to the sum total. However, these 'extra bits' are also likely to change existing interpretations of this event/person/building. This understanding of the incomplete nature of what we know and the changing interpretations that are put on what we know is not an easy understanding to develop with children and cannot be done in the abstract. However, it is central to the developing understanding of what history is and it is necessary to continue to strive to develop it further. The scenario outlined above offers an opportunity to further this development and the IT component makes a contribution in two ways.

Firstly, and quite simply, it makes it easier to update without a major potential loss in motivation, for it is likely to be a disheartening experience to have to rewrite the main story to incorporate the newly uncovered information. This is IT in its facilitating role.

The more significant contribution, however, is in the area of advancing the children's understanding of what we know and how this has come to be known. The ability to relate one new piece of information to the existing picture and to see how this complements or contradicts our existing understanding is what the process of history is about right through to the most advanced levels at which it is studied. The ongoing evaluation and re-evaluation of existing interpretations (or mental pictures) as new evidence is uncovered (or reinterpreted for its significance) is the dynamic of history.

Even where teachers have been aware of this it has not been easy to create situations in the classroom where even small steps could be made in taking this awareness a half-step forward. Here, with the use of a computer such a situation is possible to at least attempt. Many of the newsroom simulation programs (see for example, NCET, 1989) also attempt to develop this awareness, but the fact that, in the example above, it would form part of the whole topic and is based upon the children's own information makes the context more meaningful.

This is much more than just facilitating and I suggest is an example of IT enhancing the studies the children would be involved in anyway in an important area.

The assessment possibilities are considered in further detail in the final chapter where the use of a log book in which ideas and hypotheses formed and tested are kept by the children is explored. By referring to it in the final stages of the study it will become clear how the development of the hypotheses posed and the understandings developed is inter-related to the information uncovered.

Throughout the pages of this book the advantages of using the pairs of historical concepts – similarity and difference, continuity and change and cause and effect – are advanced, particularly at the planning stages. History requires that these links and comparisons be made and this is, not surprisingly, now reflected in the National Curriculum requirements. Under the heading 'Range and Depth of Historical Knowledge and Understanding' in the key elements for this age it says that children should be taught

> to describe and make links and connections between the main events and developments studied, both within and across periods.
> (History Key Elements, Key Stage 2; DFE, 1995)

The potential for doing this with this newspapers example is considerable. Using the newspapers as *both* a source of information and a way of communicating knowledge offers scope for the children to work in the style of a Victorian broadsheet newspaper and perhaps a tabloid of today. Different groups within the class (or the same group at different stages of production) could attempt to present their findings in the appropriate style and format. The use of IT here both facilitates and enhances at the same time. The children's control over both font and text size makes it very easy to reduce down anything they have written to the Victorian newspaper style and the ability to move it around as they create the page is also unlikely to pose problems. While this may just be possible by other means, it is suggested that it would be both difficult and very time consuming. The enhancement of the learning process offered by the use of IT comes from the fact that, by enabling the children to do something they could not otherwise have done, their knowledge and/or understanding of another aspect of life in a different period is taken a step further.

Inevitably comparisons will be made between the styles and questions arise – is one better than the other? If so, in what way? Why are they different? Was it just style or did the technology affect what was possible?

The consideration of what has remained the same and what has changed will almost certainly take the teacher and the children into the reasons behind the differences and the changes. This takes the investigation into the realm of exploring cause and effect – a crucial aspect of historical investigation. In this situation the IT acts as a catalyst. As such it is a very good example of the dynamic interaction between the discipline and the medium that was explored in Chapter 1 and is returned to in the final chapter.

Advertisements

Before leaving this particular area of newspapers, there is one other aspect that is worthy of the reader's consideration. It can actually be part of the newspaper but it can just as easily be free-standing: this is the use of advertisements. The rationale for the use of adverts in the teaching and learning of history is very similar to that for using newspapers. Namely, that as well as being a source of information it is also a way of children being able to communicate what they have learned and understood.

While some form of advertising has probably existed ever since goods have been presented for sale, the rapid growth that went along with industrialization, as new customers and markets were sought for the mass of goods being produced, was unprecedented. The Victorian era was therefore one when advertising really blossomed and developed. As such, it is a tremendous evidence source and can be used to gain insights into many aspects of life and across the social spectrum. It appeared in so many different forms it is impossible to list them all, but it would certainly include manufacturers' catalogues, bags and wrappings, hoardings on buildings and buses and cabs (these are often captured almost incidentally in early photographs and postcards), enamel plaques and of course in newspapers and magazines. If it was being made, it was probably being advertised!

As with newspapers there is little difficulty in obtaining copies, and even originals of some of the less valuable forms can often be loaned from Teachers'/Professional Development Centres.

A brief example illustrates how the humble advertisement might contribute to the development of the desired knowledge, skills and understanding planned for in a local history-based topic on Victorian Britain.

With the use of buildings, as considered above, as a source of information about the lives of people during this period it is quite likely that the class will have looked at the development of housing in the locality during this period. The teacher may well have encouraged the children to focus on the similarities and differences, both within the period and between today and then. Some things will have changed, but some will also have remained the same and thus the concepts of continuity and change are also explored. To consolidate and begin to communicate this knowledge and to use it to obtain a greater insight into the different levels of society,

> Pupils should be taught about the lives of men, women and children at different levels of society . . . (History, PoS, Key Stage 2; DFE, 1995)

They might be asked to create an initial 'For sale' advertisement for a house built in the Victorian years and still standing nearby. Many of the houses built in this period would have been 'state of the art' at the time they were built. The adverts seeking to find buyers for them would have reflected this in both the language used and the features highlighted, like water supply and sanitation, heating and lighting, etc., coach house, or servant accommodation, and it would be a challenging task to recreate such a positive picture of something almost certainly not regarded in this way by children living in the 1990s. Another group within the class could draw up a similar estate agent-type advert for the same property today. 'In need of some modernization', 'cellar/attic room available for conversion', 'many original features' might well feature as a positive picture is sought. The price difference itself would normally give rise to some interesting and often lively discussion!

As the children will be aware, most estate agents' advertisements today feature a picture of the property. Sketches, or better still, photographs would contribute to the realistic nature of the advert being created. As with many of the ideas explored in this and subsequent chapters, all this could, and has been, done without using IT. However, by using one of the many text and graphics manipulation packages most schools now have, two particular gains are made. At the basic level the end product is likely to look more like what it is supposed to be. The reason for this is not simply to do with presentation, but rather because the ability to manipulate the words and position of the words is more likely to encourage the pursuit of the desired outcome.

However, in terms of the children's development in historical understanding, it is the opportunity to update and modify previous impressions as new knowledge and understanding is acquired that is of greater importance. If, for example, the task above was set up for the children (probably in groups) quite early in the topic, they would commence on their advertisement with some but rather limited knowledge. As the topic progressed new information arising from a further visit, a conversation with an older member of the community or from an input made by the teacher on, say, sanitation would begin to inform and modify initial impressions. As was explored in the newspaper example above, IT provides the medium through which this can be reflected upon and incorporated into the developing understanding without constantly having to consider starting again with all its likely consequences in the sphere of motivation. As has been outlined above, one of the most important realizations for children studying history is that we do not know everything and there are always gaps in our knowledge of the past. A key skill of the historian is being able to identify what he/she needs to know and then to identify where they might pursue their enquiries further. The framework of the advert provides a very good context for children to develop these skills in a meaningful way. The power given by IT to manipulate the presentation enables the new information to be merged with the old and so to take the understanding a stage further. This ability to communicate this developing understanding is now a key part of this subject.

> Pupils should be taught to communicate their knowledge and understanding of history in a variety of ways. . . . (History, Key Elements, Key Stage 2; DFE, 1995)

Houses was just the example chosen here; within this same Victorian/local study topic it could easily have been advertisements for the bicycle, the water closet or Thomas Cook's early excursions.

Just before leaving these newspaper/advertisements examples one element in both is worth exploring a little further to illustrate how the present and future developments in IT will continue to feed into and contribute to history in schools. The use of photographs in the above examples was suggested as offering something extra than the sketch or drawing made on the visit. The traditional photo could certainly be used as the centre piece of an advert or newspaper report, with text being added as appropriate. However, the technology is now available to schools (which is rather different from merely being available) to enter the photograph itself into the computer program, where it too can be manipulated. This can be done by either using a scanner or more successfully by using one of the Ion cameras (i.e. Canon) which take the photo on to a disk. The photo can then be transferred into almost any of the art/drawing programs that schools already have, with no further developing required. At present few primary schools have either scanners or such cameras, but it is likely that there is one at the Teachers'/Professional Development Centre that can be borrowed. It is also worth noting that most high schools will have a scanner and increasingly an Ion camera to support their own Information Technology courses and if local relationships are close enough help may be available from here. Where I have heard of such co-operation, the loan of the camera has usually included the loan of a helpful and knowledgeable older pupil from the high school as well! Once the photo (and the camera referred to will take 25–50 photos on the one disk, which can then be used again) has been transferred into the computer it is available to be worked upon – increased in size, zoomed in on, parts highlighted or cut out for special features. Of course it is also now possible to annotate the photo or add explanatory labels.

As was stated above, this exploration has been concerned with new ways of undertaking activities that can and have been taking place in primary schools without the use of IT. However, the freedom that is given to zoom in, resize, cut and paste, annotate, etc. by this technological development will almost certainly lead to more questions being asked, more hypotheses being posed and more avenues of enquiry being opened up. The use of scanners and Ion cameras are small-scale examples of the claims made by Papert (1980) in relation to the way IT can open up the learning situation for children.

Developing an IT capability

The contributions being made to each child's developing IT capability by being involved in these activities in his/her history topics are considered in greater depth in the final chapter. The sections of the IT requirements for this Key Stage which have been touched upon in the above examples are however worth just noting here.

Pupils should be given opportunities to

a. use IT to explore and solve problems in the context of work across a variety of subjects

b. use IT to further their understanding of information that they have retrieved and processed

c. discuss their experiences of using IT and assess its value to their working practices

d. investigate parallels with the use of IT in the wider world, consider the effects of such uses, and compare them with other methods. (IT PoS, Key Stage 2; DFE, 1995)

It can be seen that creating situations whereby children will have opportunities to use IT in history-based topics such as those considered above creates a context in which this capability can be further developed.

Conclusion

This chapter has sought to explore through specific examples how IT might contribute to the teaching and learning of history within the context of a popular topic based in Victorian Britain and the locality. It has been suggested throughout that IT facilitated and further enhanced the activities that were undertaken. By doing so the children's development in the field of history is taken forward in a way that would be neither easy nor at times possible without the use of IT. However, as was also seen, there were occasions when the IT factor was moving beyond these two roles and was, or had the potential to, act as a catalyst in a way that helped the learning situation to develop a dynamic of its own, thus opening up new avenues and lines of enquiry. The important thing to note here is that it was the children who were the 'agents' that the catalyst acted upon. The response of the teacher, who will always be responsible for managing the learning environment, is of the greatest significance when this occurs. The pedagogical implications immediately become very significant and one is immediately taken back to the central issue explored in Chapter 1 in relation to one's own philosophy of education and the position of the child in this. Quite rightly, the teacher has an agenda that is wider than developments within one curriculum area on one particular day. This wider agenda is likely to include the implications for classroom organization, equal opportunities and the way these might manifest themselves in terms of differentiation and access, of continuity and progression across the curriculum, to mention just a few. These cannot and must not be sidestepped. The successful addressing of these is central to the success of the ideas and suggestions presented above. These issues are returned to and explored in greater detail in Chapter 5. The issue of assessment is also considered in some depth there in relation to both the history knowledge, skills and understanding being developed and also with regard to the development of each child's IT capability.

References

Arkell, T. (1989) Analysing Victorian census data on computer. *Teaching History*, **54**, 18–25.

DES (1985) *History in the Primary and Secondary Years: An HMI View*. London: HMSO.

DES (1989) *Aspects of Primary Practice: The Teaching and Learning of History*. London: HMSO.

DES (1991a) *History in the National Curriculum.* London: HMSO.

DES (1991b) *History Non-statutory Guidance.* London: HMSO.

DES (1991c) *Aspects of Primary Practice: The Teaching and Learning of Information Technology.* London: HMSO.

DFE (1995) *Key Stages 1 and 2 of the National Curriculum.* London: HMSO.

Keith, C. (1991) *A Teacher's Guide to Using Listed Buildings.* London: English Heritage.

Knight, P. and Timmins, G. (1986) Using databases in history teaching. *Journal of Computer Assisted Learning,* **2**(2), 93–101.

NCC/SEAC (1993a) *The National Curriculum and Its Assessment: An Interim Report by Sir Ron Dearing.* London: HMSO.

NCC/SEAC (1993b) *The National Curriculum and Its Assessment: Final Report.* London: HMSO.

NCET (1989) *History in the Headlines.* Coventry: NCET.

OFSTED (1993) *Curriculum Organisation and Classroom Practice in Primary Schools: A Follow-up Report.* London: OFSTED.

OFSTED (1994) *Primary Matters: A Discussion on Teaching and Learning in Primary Schools.* London: OFSTED.

Papert, S. (1980) *Mindstorms: Children, Computers and Powerful Ideas.* Hemel Hempstead, Herts: Harvester Press.

Papert, S. (1993) *The Children's Machine: Rethinking School in the Age of the Computer.* Hemel Hempstead, Herts: Harvester Press.

Parker, C. and Smart, L. (1992) *Making Links.* Coventry: NCET.

Purkiss, S. (1993) *A Teacher's Guide to Using School Buildings.* London: English Heritage.

Ross, A. (1983) Microcomputers and local history work in a primary school. *Teaching History,* **35**, 82–85.

Smart, L. (1988) The database as a catalyst. *Journal of Computer Assisted Learning,* **4**(3), 140–149.

Smart, L. (1992) 'Databases, history and young historians', in J. Lodge (ed.), *Computer Datahandling in the Primary School.* London: Fulton.

CHAPTER 3
Invaders and Settlers

Romans, Anglo-Saxons and Vikings! Few children who have passed through the British primary school system can have failed to have come across at least one of these groups of people. Along with dinosaurs and cavemen they are old-established favourites and the number of schools that have never had a set of R.J. Unstead's *From Cavemen to Vikings* on their shelves must be very small indeed.

However, the way in which these and other historical periods and people were studied in primary schools was found seriously wanting when last reported upon (HMI, 1989).

> The standards of work achieved in history, whether taught separately or as part of topic work, were very disappointing. In only one in five infant schools and departments and one in three junior schools and departments were standards judged to be satisfactory or better. (para. 11)

In a very disparaging tone HMI note,

> . . . in infant and lower junior classes . . . teaching about the past was often confined to stories about dinosaurs, cavemen and the Romans. (para. 13; DES, 1989)

While dinosaurs, and indeed cavemen, have all but disappeared from the history curriculum since it became national, the Romans have had their status enhanced and the Saxons and the Vikings have been elevated to a similar level. All three now feature in the statutory orders for this curriculum area (DFE, 1995).

It was not just the limited choice of content and the absence of adequate planning that so concerned HMI, but also the fact that so many teachers lacked an understanding of the importance of the *processes* of history. The importance and significance of this HMI document (DES, 1989) was considered in Chapter 1, where it was seen that the National Curriculum requirements for history that followed some two years later (DES, 1991a) were a direct response to the situation they had reported upon.

The Non-statutory Guidance (NSG), sent to every school soon after the original history National Curriculum of 1991, was written to guide and support teachers as they sought to meet the new requirements for this subject.

The NSG clearly attempts to establish the importance of the 'how we know' alongside the 'what we know' of the past.

Under the heading 'The Purposes of School History' it stated:

> History can mean two things. The past, and the study of the past. The past influences all aspects of our lives. It shapes the customs and beliefs of the communities to which we belong. Learning about the past and the methods used to study it helps pupils make sense of the world in which they live.
>
> There are two main aims of school history:
>
> to help pupils develop a sense of identity through learning about the development of Britain, Europe and the world;
> to introduce pupils to what is involved in understanding and interpreting the past.
>
> A strong sense of *why* [original emphasis] history is being taught should pervade all curriculum planning, influencing the selection of content and methods of teaching. (History NSG, p. B1; DES, 1991b)

So, whereas the historical topics themselves might be recognizable to anyone who was at primary school in the pre-National Curriculum decades, the way these studies are now undertaken should be noticeably and significantly different.

The absence of the non-statutory guidance, or any guidance at all with the revised 1995 version of the history National Curriculum is, however, a serious cause for concern. It is a result of the desire to reduce the amount of documentation sent to schools and all blanket decisions of this nature run the risk of including the useful along with the superfluous. One can only hope that once the dust has settled on the new model there will be selective and quality support provided. There is little doubt that the National Curriculum has made a very significant contribution to many teachers' grasp and understanding of what constitutes good history and of the central position of the process of the inquiry to this subject. Although there is evidence of considerable progress having been made (OFSTED, 1993), there is still a tremendous amount of consolidation that needs to be done. The ongoing need for *points of reference*, as the original NSG provided for teachers, remains. It will be interesting to see how this issue, for it is a wider one and applies to other subject areas as well, will be addressed in the post-1995 years.

The greatest complaint about the initial National Curriculum requirements for history at KS2 was the number of topics that had to be covered. Sir Ron Dearing was left in no doubt about this point in the responses he received from primary school teachers during his consultation exercise in 1993 (NCC/SEAC, 1993b). To reduce the the number of topics and to attempt to help create situations where more in-depth studies could be undertaken meant decisions had to be made as to what to take out and what to leave in.

Invaders and Settlers survived this pruning exercise with very little change at all. The significant feature is the increased emphasis in the revised model to focus on *one* of the three and *to study it in greater depth*. The in-depth emphasis almost certainly reflects the points identified in the annual OFSTED report of 1993 (para. 46), where concern was expressed about the sacrificing of in-depth study to ensure the required breadth of coverage.

It is appropriate therefore to start with a look at what the present requirements are, as the examples which follow arise from them. As with the previous and following chapters on Victorian Britain and the Tudor Period, the intention is to suggest and illustrate how the use of IT can contribute to the development of the knowledge, skills and understanding that teachers will be seeking to achieve in their history-based studies. An attempt will also be made to identify and explore how, at the same time, this use will also contribute to the further development of the children's IT capability.

The National Curriculum requirements for the teaching of history at this Key Stage are known as a Programme of Study and consist of two parts. The first part is the Key Elements and these are common to all the history topics undertaken. The second part consists of the details of the areas or aspects to be studied, the content, of each topic. Together they are intended to ensure the development of the necessary knowledge, skills and understanding of history. At the end of the Key Stage this is assessed in relation to the level descriptions of the Attainment Target for this subject. First then, the Elements required for KS2 history:

Key Elements

The Key Elements outlined below are closely related and should be developed through the Study Units, as appropriate. Not all the Key Elements need to be developed in each Study Unit.

Pupils should be taught:

1. **Chronology**
    a. to place the events, people and changes in the periods studied within a chronological framework;
    b. to use dates and terms relating to the passing of time, including ancient, modern, BC, AD, century and decade, and terms that define different periods, *e.g. Tudor, Victorian.*

2. **Range and Depth of Historical Knowledge and Understanding**
    a. about characteristic features of particular periods and societies, including the ideas, beliefs and attitudes of people in the past, and the experiences of men and women; and about the social, cultural, religious and ethnic diversity of the societies studied.
    b. to describe and identify reasons for and results of historical events, situations, and changes in the periods studied.

    c. to describe and make links between the main events, situations and changes both within and across periods.

3. **Interpretations of History**
   a. to identify and give reasons for different ways in which the past is represented and interpreted.

4. **Historical Enquiry**
   a. how to find out about aspects of the periods studied, from a range of resources of information, including documents and printed sources, artefacts, pictures and photographs, music, and buildings and sites.
   b. to ask and answer questions, and to select and record information relevant to a topic.

5. **Organisation and Communication**
   a. to recall, select and organise historical information, including dates and terms;
   b. the terms necessary to describe the periods and topics studied, including court, monarch, parliament, nation, civilisations, invasion, conquest, settlement, conversion, slavery, trade, industry, law.
   c. to communicate their knowledge and understanding of history in a variety of ways, including structured narratives and descriptions.
   (History, Key Elements, Key Stage 2; DFE, 1995)

These Key Elements are what is required to be taught irrespective of the actual content matter being studied, and one can see how the emphasis is placed on the *process* of historical investigation and the communication of the results of this. This is then complemented by details of the content matter, the *knowledge* that is to be taught. For Invaders and Settlers this consists of:

Study Unit 1. Romans, Anglo-Saxons and Vikings in Britain

Pupils should be taught about the history of the British Isles from 55 BC to the early eleventh century, and the ways in which British society was shaped by different peoples. They should be given opportunities to study, in greater depth, ONE of the Romans, the Anglo-Saxons, or the Vikings.

1. Pupils should be taught **in outline** about the following:
   a the Roman conquest and the occupation of Britain,
   b the arrival and settlement of the Anglo-Saxons,
   c Viking raids and settlement.

2. They should be taught **in greater depth** about ONE of the following:
   a. Romans
       – the Roman conquest and its impact on Britain *e.g. Boudicca and resistance to Roman rule, the extent to which life in Celtic Britain was influenced by Roman rule and settlement, the end of Imperial rule.*
       – everyday life *e.g. houses and homelife, work, religion.*
       – the legacy of Roman rule *e.g. place names and settlement patterns, Roman remains, including artefacts, roads and buildings.*

OR

b. Anglo-Saxons

- the arrival and settlement of the Anglo-Saxons and their impact on England *e.g. early settlement, the conversion of the Anglo-Saxons to Christianity, King Alfred and Anglo-Saxon resistance to the Vikings.*
- everyday life *e.g. houses and home life, work, religion.*
- the legacy of settlement *e.g. place names, and settlement patterns, myths and legends, Anglo-Saxon remains, including artefacts and buildings.*

OR

c. Vikings

- Viking raids and settlement and their impact on the British Isles *e.g. their settlement in different parts of the British Isles, King Alfred and Anglo-Saxon resistance to the Vikings.*
- everyday life *e.g. houses and home life, work, religion.*
- the legacy of settlement *e.g. place names, and settlement patterns, myths and legends, Viking remains including artefacts and buildings.*
  (History, Key Stage. 2; DFE, 1995)

(All emphases, italics, etc. are as found in the statutory orders. The words in italics are not statutory and are for guidance only.)

The Key Elements and the requirements listed for study unit are intended to balance each other. Taken together, it is intended that the *skills* and the *knowledge* will effectively develop the *understanding* that must remain the ultimate aim.

In the following examples specific aspects of this programme of study will be focused upon. The examples used will seek to explore how IT can make a contribution to the development of the required historical knowledge, skills and understanding that the teacher would be aiming for. Throughout this book the examples used have attempted to show that there are times when the appropriate use of IT *facilitates* the realization of these aims. Secondly, in some examples it has been suggested that there are times when the use of IT *enhances* what might be achieved. No attempt is made to claim that other methods could not produce a similar result, simply that the appropriate use of IT at the appropriate time can lead to it being done more easily and in some cases, better. Finally it will be argued there are times when IT enables things to be achieved in the classroom that would be very difficult, if not impossible to achieve without it. It is this final dimension that is explored in greater detail in this chapter. Can the use of IT really take school-based history teaching into areas and on to higher levels than was previously possible? These are big claims but it is necessary to remind ourselves that these are no different from those made by Papert (1980) when computers first became a reality in the school situation and their potential impact was first considered.

As the references supporting Chapter 1 show, this potential has been constantly hinted at or referred to throughout the 1980s. Perhaps the first decade of IT in schools was one in which the innovation had to become accepted. If a second stage of development is indeed now underway, maybe some of the earlier visionary ideas may move into the mainstream. The reader must decide whether the examples and interpretations made in the following pages offer any evidence to support whether this is, or is likely to become, the case.

In classroom and in-service education for teachers (INSET) course discussions, and also at conferences one often hears teachers comment positively on the use they now make of artefacts, buildings and oral history to enable children to work with primary sources. This is encouraging evidence of the way the National Curriculum has had a positive impact on teachers' understanding of the subject. However, inevitably it always seems, someone adds that this is fine when you are doing the 1930s to the Present Day or Victorians but what about when you do the Invaders? There is no arguing with the fact that some periods of history are easier to resource on a broader base than others and there can be little doubt that this makes it easier for the teacher to create situations where the children can be involved in the process of historical enquiry itself. What teachers feeling these frustrations need to remember and acknowledge is that this is also the case for *all* historians operating at any level right through to the professional. The scholar studying the role and position of women in Roman society will not have access to the same range and amount of evidence that a colleague studying women in Victorian society has at his/her disposal. And, without doubt, the latter will certainly wish they had more at some time in his/her studies. Of course this is both part of the attraction and the frustration of the discipline itself!

The examples and suggestions that are developed in the following pages seek to explore how, and where, IT might make a contribution to helping teachers address some of these difficulties. In particular, an attempt will be made to see how and where IT can make a contribution to the very real difficulties of giving children access to the wide range of sources as listed in the National Curriculum Key Elements (see above) which, it is worth reminding ourselves, merely reflects what good history has been about for many years now. It is important to remember that that this wide range of sources is not something that is simply desirable in its own right. It is only by creating situations where children have access to such that they can become involved in the *process* of historical enquiry.

This is clearly captured in Point 4 of the Key Elements for Key Stage 2:

4. **Historical Enquiry** (pupils should be taught)
   a. how to find out about aspects of the past from a range of resources of

information, including artefacts, pictures and photographs, adults talking about their past, written sources and buildings and sites.

b. to ask and answer questions about the past.

(Key Elements, KS2; DFE, 1995)

Unless the first part of this section is realized, namely the opportunity to work with *a range of resources* the aim of developing the ability to *select* those most appropriate to further the investigation has little chance of success. The greatest loss, however, is almost certainly the development of the ability to *ask and answer questions*, the very basis of the subject itself (Collingwood, 1946).

How then might the use of IT in a history topic on Invaders and Settlers enable teachers to create situations where access to a wider range of source material is available than otherwise might be possible? At the outset this attempt must be put in the context of availability and access to source material generally. For several years in the mid-1970s I undertook a topic on the Second World War with a focus on the Home Front with my class. In response to my requests for support from parents I received enough tin helmets and gas masks for the whole class to be fitted out! Ration books, identity cards, newspapers, service ephemera (including newspapers, demob papers, cook books and maps), blackout curtains and more came into school freely. At another stage in the topic there were also few difficulties in setting up face-to-face interviews with people who had been in the services, experienced the Blitz, been evacuated and who remembered the VE celebrations. Twenty years later none of these would be quite as easy and in another twenty some would quite obviously be all but impossible. The Imperial War Museum now produces replicas of much of the paper-based materials and photopacks and tapes with interviews of people who lived through this period can also be obtained. The point being established here is that availability and access to source material for any period is not static and the passage of time begins to affect this availability.

The other major factor which has a bearing on access to source material is of course its location. Aztec or Maya temples, Egyptian pyramids, city remains in Benin or the Indus valley or, nearer at home Hadrian's Wall, Hampton Court and York are all accessible, but unfortunately other mundane factors, like cost, come into play when availability is considered.

Are replicas and reproductions and photographs of places and artifacts acceptable and worthwhile? It obviously depends upon the purpose they are being used for. A replica Roman coin would be of little use to a historian exploring metal use and techniques in the period but the same replica could be of use in another context relating to dates and names on the coin. The use of replicas and photographs/reproductions of primary source material must always be viewed with circumspection, but it is acceptable and accepted in historical enquiries, at all levels. There are certain criteria which must be satisfied with regard to accuracy and authenticity, quality of reproduction, etc., and any teacher using reproductions must be careful to explore these factors before using them with the children. I have, for example, some serious reservations about some of the photographs presented for use as source material in the various packs that appeared on the market in the immediate wake of the history National Curriculum.

Having acknowledged reservations and the need for care in using reproductions and photographs of scarce and/or inaccessible source material, there is little doubt that it is often the only realistic way that children in schools can have access to them.

Earlier in this chapter it was argued that it is necessary for children to have this access to as wide a range of source material as possible if they are to develop the desired historical skills. Can IT make a significant contribution here? The example below seeks to show that the answer is very definitely yes. It attempts to show how the use of IT and particularly the recent developments in CD-ROM technology and its increasing availability in schools can enable children to have access to previously inaccessible source material. By so doing, it will be claimed, it opens up the possibilities of children being able to be as involved in the *processes* of historical enquiry when they are studying the Invaders and Settlers as when they are studying the more recent past.

Romans, Anglo-Saxons and Vikings

The National Curriculum requirements, as listed earlier in this chapter, will be the framework for studies undertaken in this period although the way these are tackled will vary from school to school. However, one of the reasons why OFSTED (1995) were able to report sound and steady progress in the field of primary history was due to more effective planning. The dual emphasis of the what and the how of history that emerged and then became the statutory orders meant that this needed to be built into the planning. The guidance offered by the NSG (DES, 1991b) encouraged teachers to adopt the Key Question approach to their planning in history. This was by no means a new model but its use within, and increasingly beyond, the humanities has certainly become much more widespread in recent years. (For a wider discussion of this model and its application see Parker and Smart, 1992.) Teachers adopting this model and working to the programme of study for this unit might identify the following questions to build into their plans.

Who were the Romans/Anglo-Saxons, Vikings?
Why did they come to Britain?

> Where did they come from?
> When did they come?
> How did they get here?
> What were they like? their clothes, houses, food, and other aspects of their lives.

A basic framework can be built around these but few children could tackle these questions without adding a little more structure. It is suggested that this can be provided by using the very useful pairs of historical concepts, *similarity and difference, continuity and change,* and *cause and effect.*

In the programme of study for Invaders and Settlers considered earlier in this chapter, it was seen how the revised orders of 1995 request that teachers focus on one of the three groups of people and in the following it is the Vikings that are considered. Because the purpose here is to explore the use and contribution of IT to the children's development in history, just one aspect of this topic has been chosen to focus on here —everyday life.

> pupils should be taught about everyday life *e.g. houses and home life, work and religion.* (DFE, 1995)

The examples used throughout the rest of this chapter draw freely upon a topic on Invaders and Settlers undertaken by a teacher and his class of 7- to 8-year-olds. Sharing a common interest in exploring the contribution IT might make to teaching and learning in the primary classroom, we agreed to co-operate to explore this agenda within this history-based topic and further details are given below. Here it is sufficient to establish that within this class one group of children had chosen to explore what everyday life was like for Viking people.

The Key Question and paired concept approach was adopted and the following framework arose from initial discussions with the children in the group.

- What kind of houses did Vikings live in?
    - How were they like ours and how were they different?
    - Why were some things the same and some different?
    - Why do you think that was so?
- Did all the Vikings live in the same type of house?
    - What was different/what was the same?
    - Why do you think this was so?
- What did they have inside their houses?
    - What things do we have that they have?
    - What things did they have that we don't?
    - What things did they have that we have?
    - Why do you think some things are different and some the same?

- Does the house and its contents help us to understand more about the people who lived in it?
  - What can it tell us about the men, the women and the children?

The children in this example were aware through their previous studies that they would be expected to be able to answer the inevitable question from their classmates and teacher:

How do you know that?
Why do you think that?

The awareness that the information, ideas or hypotheses presented would need to be able to be supported if challenged is one that is increasingly likely to permeate history in schools as the foundations now being laid in KS1 (OFSTED, 1993) are developed into KS2 and KS3.

And also, of the greatest importance, the children were asked to identify to themselves what questions haven't been answered.

What do we still need to try and find out?
Where could be go to find out more?

These final questions are very important in helping children realize that there is so much that not only do we not know now, but it is very likely that we never will. The incomplete nature of historical knowledge and under-standing is central to the discipline itself. If one subscribes to the 'intellectual honesty' of the Bruner model of curriculum design (see below), one needs to enable children to become aware of this. It is something that the vast numbers of history books produced for schools have singularly failed to do.

Thus a situation is created whereby the task is clearly identified. The outcome was agreed to be a wall display which the group would talk to the rest of the class about. The framework of questions (above) was included in the display itself so that any reader could easily see what the children had set out to do and, as it was developed later, to see where they sought their information and which bits of this information they had thought relevant to include in their presentation.

Before turning to examine this specific example in more detail it is useful to place it in the wider context of recent developments in primary school history.

There is little doubt that this task, from the initial questions right through to the presentation, could be undertaken without any use of IT. Indeed in those classrooms where HMI (DES, 1989) identified good history teaching, if the topic had been Invaders and Settlers it is quite likely that it would have been tackled in a similar way to the above but without an IT component. However, I suggest that the fact that the good practice examples in the HMI report (DES, 1989) were all local history must not be overlooked. There is little doubt that the National Curriculum has furthered many teachers' understanding of what good history teaching should include, especially a greatly increased awareness of the 'how we know' element. The steady permeation of the quite explicit message contained in the Non-statutory Orders (DES, 1991b),

> Learning about the past and the methods used to study it helps pupils to make sense of the world in which they live.
>
> There are two main aims of school history: to help pupils develop a sense of identity through learning about the development of Britain, Europe and the world; to introduce pupils to what is involved in understanding and interpreting the past. (NC History NSG, B1; DES, 1991b)

is increasingly found in primary history teaching in the mid-1990s. The concern expressed earlier about just where teachers might find a similar common reference point in the absence of any guidance in the revised model of 1995 remains.

The difficulty, as was identified above and is now realized by most primary teachers, is how to involve the children in the process of enquiry when primary evidence and resources are so much less accessible than they are for the recent and local past. Unless progress can be made and support offered here one fears that when HMI or OFSTED next reports on primary history and details good examples, Invaders and Settlers, Greeks, Benin and other more distant history, in both time and place, will not feature.

Are there any signs that this support might be forthcoming? Increasingly since the mid-1980s school history books have moved away from merely presenting information about a historical period, person, object or other without some attempt to use evidence to support the information. The New History movement and particularly the School Council (1978, 1980) have been particularly influential in this development, which has been continued into the 1990s by the Nuffield Primary History Project (1995). Since 1991 many publishers have responded to the commercial opportunities provided by the needs of over 20,000 primary schools for materials to support the new National Curriculum requirements. The number of resource packs, offering books and worksheet materials for children, guidelines for teachers and assessment/recording sheets based on the attainment targets, was on a scale only previously seen by the era of the Schools Council packs of the early 1970s. As with all 'packs', and for any curriculum area, the contents were a variable mixture of high, sound and dismal quality. However, in those produced to support the new history curriculum there was a very definite acknowledgement and attempt to cater for the second part of the agenda as identified in the quotation from the History NSG (DES, 1991b):

to introduce pupils to what is involved in understanding and interpreting the past.

This often took the form of a photograph or poster of a piece of primary evidence. Examples include a photograph of a section of the bas-relief on Trajan's Column in Rome alongside a modern drawing of what a Roman galley looked like, or a photograph of the Sutton Hoo ship alongside the statement that Saxon boats were of a shallow draft. These developments in 'school' history books are a very definite step forward, acknowledging that it is no longer adequate or acceptable to present the products of the historical enquiry without at least alerting the reader to how this came to be arrived at. The books from which the above two examples are taken indicate progress but are still seriously deficient in contributing to that wider aim of developing children's understanding of the methods of history. The missing ingredient here is the acknowledgement that the bass relief, the finds in the excavation or whatever have had to be *interpreted*, they have not spoken for themselves.

The concern that must remain is that, even with the development above, too many school history books continue to present as fact what is usually no more than an 'As far as we know. . .' situation. It is difficult to see why authors are not more prepared to say 'As far as we know. . .' or 'We think that. . .', whether it be that 'The Anglo-Saxons didn't like living in towns' or 'Vikings held their religious ceremonies outdoors because they believed evil spirits could not interfere there'. This then opens up the opportunity to continue, 'We think this because. . .'.

It has been argued (Lawlor, 1991) that this would simply confuse children and it is only when they have built up a sound knowledge base that they can be exposed to and develop an understanding of the uncertain nature and varying interpretations of historical knowledge. There are several objections to such a standpoint. Firstly, it is dishonest to present something as known when it is quite simply not so. Secondly, it is not history that is being taught, for the tentative and changing nature of what counts as knowledge is one of the features that makes it a distinctive discipline. Thirdly, the understanding of the processes of history, of *how* we know as well as *what*, is fundamental to this subject. And finally, quite simply, it underestimates what children are capable of. The realization of the significance of teacher expectation on child performance is certainly not new (Rosenthal and Jacobson, 1968; Mortimore *et al.*, 1989; HMI, 1989, 1990) and is still one of the major messages from OFSTED in the mid-1990s (OFSTED, 1993, 1994).

It is now over 30 years since Jerome Bruner (1963, 1966) presented his ideas that any subject could be studied in an intellectually honest way, at any level, as long as the nature of the discipline was understood. A key feature of this nature is its truth establishing methods (Rogers, 1987) which is different for each discipline and usually gives rise to each discipline's distinctive concepts, i.e. the fair test in science. The influence of Bruner's ideas and particularly his development of the spiral model of curriculum planning has had a major impact on British primary education. The recently developed National Curriculum is clearly heavily influenced by this idea, and nowhere more so than in history.

A re-examination of the Key Elements listed earlier in this chapter shows quite clearly and unequivocally that the model of history that now forms the National Curriculum model is one based upon intellectual honesty. Children from the earliest years of schooling are required to be involved in the process as well as the content of history.

To return to the specific example, it will be seen that it explores how the use of an appropriate CD-ROM enabled a teacher to create situations whereby children could have access to otherwise inaccessible source material in such a way that they had the necessary degree of control over it to use it in their own investigations. These issues of appropriateness, control and use are central and it is felt that these are most effectively explored within the context that this example provides.

The questions the children used for their investigation into everyday life of Viking society were detailed above but are worth restating here.

- What kind of houses did Vikings live in?
    - How were they like ours and how were they different?
    - Why were some things the same and some different?
    - Why do you think that was so?
- Did all the Vikings live in the same type of house?
    - What was different/what was the same?
    - Why do you think this was so?
- What did they have inside their houses?
    - What things do we have that they have?
    - What things did they have that we don't?
    - What things did they have that we have?
    - Why do you think some things are different and some the same?
- Does the house and its contents help us to understand more about the people who lived in it?
    - What can it tell us about the men, the women and the children?
- How do you know that?
- Why do you think that?

And, as was noted above, the children would be asked to identify to themselves what questions haven't been answered.

What do we still need to try and find out?
Where could we go to find out more?

This example calls freely upon a small-scale research project which sought to explore if, and how, the use of CD-ROMs in the primary classroom could contribute to the development of the skills of historical enquiry by giving children increased and easier access to primary source material. The full details of this classroom research are detailed elsewhere (Smart and Taylor, 1995), but a few further details help to create the context. The school was in an inner-London borough, the children were in a class of 30 coming mainly from the immediate high/low-rise estate and were aged 7 to 8 years old. The study was certainly not substantial enough to offer anything more than informed comments and observations, but these do provide some interesting insights into how the use of this particular aspect of IT, the CD-ROM can contribute to the teaching and learning of history with this age range.

In relation to the questions that were guiding the children's investigations the first, and central one addressed was

What kind of houses did Vikings live in?

There were no problems finding several books that had pictures of a Viking house and the children quickly found these. One was obviously an artist's impression (although it was not acknowledged as such) and the other looked like a photograph of a reconstruction building (again unacknowledged). The question was asked 'How do we know they are right?' Being aware from earlier work that the Vikings arrived in Britain over a thousand years ago, the children spent some time in discussion and concluded that it was not impossible but not very likely that any of the original houses had survived, so how did the person who had written the book know they looked like this? Where's her evidence? This questioning attitude with regard to the un-supported printed word or picture had been cultivated by the teacher and, it is suggested, is necessary in helping children develop an understanding of the processes of history.

Where could the children have gone to investigate this central question? In a moment it will be seen how they used the Viking World CD-ROM (Past Forward, 1993) to explore this, but what other alternatives were available? Quite simply the answer is very few. A museum visit to Jorvick would have been ideal but quite out of the question in terms of time and finance; further use of books from the school and local library were possibilities and these avenues were explored. However the ones that were found that had the required supporting information were totally inappropriate in terms of vocabulary and presentation. They had been written for a much older audience with more advanced comprehension and information retrieval skills. The TV programme watched the previous week on the Vikings was another possible avenue and had certainly had houses in, but the same questions remained; if they weren't original buildings how did the film maker know?

This is a scenario many primary teachers are increasingly likely to be able to identify with in their history topics. The need for materials that do not prevent the children's limited vocabulary and reading skills allowing them access to information and concepts that are well within their grasp.

CD-ROMS — MORE OF THE SAME OR SOMETHING DIFFERENT?

This class had been used to having a computer in their classroom ever since they had entered the school and were confident users of the word processing program. They had also used different drawing and painting packages, some maths games and had used a database to support previous topics. Although the classes had had to be reorganized for the current year, there were a group of children who had also previously used a CD-ROM, though not extensively.

The observations made related to the children's specific investigations into Viking houses. Did the use of IT in this CD-ROM format contribute to the children's enquiries by enabling them to access materials that were unavailable and inaccessible by other means? Secondly, and just as important, did it present this information in such a manner that was appropriate in terms of vocabulary and reading skills? If the latter criterion was not met, the advantage gained was nullified and one is back with the situation of the books mentioned above. If these two were met satisfactorily did they create a situation whereby the children's ability to ask questions and pose hypotheses of this information was released? As was stated in an earlier chapter it is not the intention of this book to evaluate specific software and here the focus is on exploring and reflecting upon the possibilities and potential of the CD-ROM, still a relatively new medium. The observations made here are based on one specific program, *The World of the Vikings* (Past Forward, 1993). A more detailed evaluation of this particular CD-ROM is to found in the full report on this research project (Smart and Taylor, 1995).

One now returns to the investigation this group of children were involved in and their brief to attempt to find out

What kind of houses did the Vikings live in? — and how do we know?

The children, a mixed-ability group of 7- to 8-year-olds consisting of two boys and two girls, looked at the collection of CD-ROMs. They considered using the encyclopaedia *Encarta* (Microsoft) but, not surprisingly, chose *The World of the Vikings* to continue their enquiries, which had so far proved unproductive using other resources.

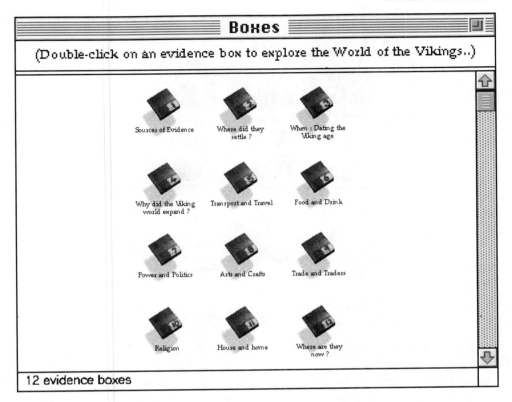

Figure 3.1

Could the use of this CD-ROM provide a situation whereby they could access the information they had identified they needed for their enquiries? And secondly, would this be available in a way they could exercise some control over it (i.e. take notes, print out, photocopy, record) so that they could move to the final stage of being able to use it within their specific investigation?

ACCESSING AND CONTROLLING THE INFORMATION

This section follows the children through their early use of *The World of the Vikings* CD-ROM to explore these issues.

Once the disk was loaded, the attractive opening scene was replaced by one showing 12 (six at a time) cardboard evidence boxes, each with a title (see Fig. 3.1). All the boxes are initially closed. The titles are brief and concise and posed no problem. The temptation to point and click (that is, move the mouse

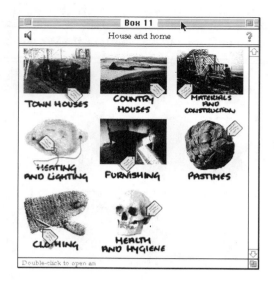

Figure 3.2

pointer and click the mouse button) was irresistible and some time was spent doing just this. This was certainly not wasted time but was in fact very productive in getting the feel of the program; how one moved back and forward in it, how one turned the voice commentary on and off, why some words were highlighted and what happened when you clicked them, etc. What was interesting at this initial stage was that these 7- to 8-year-olds did almost exactly what the class teacher and I had done when we looked at the program for the first time! They quite simply explored it.

Ever since the earliest evaluations of the contribution of IT in the primary classroom were written (i.e. Garland, 1982; Maddison, 1982; Kelly, 1984), the power of the computer to motivate, stimulate and even excite has been a constant feature and this was certainly so at this stage. Eventually the group focused its attention on the task of the Viking House and set about using the program and their rudimentary understanding of it to try to further their investigation.

They returned to the evidence boxes (see Fig. 3.1), talked through the titles again and opened the one entitled House and Home. Having done so they were presented with another screen (Fig. 3.2) with eight aspects of house and home life presented for consideration. The choice became 'which one first' rather than merely 'which one', because all eight were examined. What was impressive after this initial, and understandable, desire to explore everything and open every box and window, was the group's ability to discriminate. In discussion it was decided that the windows on Town Houses and Country Houses would be looked at first and that Heating and Lighting, Furnishing, and Pastimes might be useful later. The title Materials and Construction proved difficult to read and was obviously not understood by the group and led to the first 'Sir, what does this mean. . .'. His explanation unpicked and re-presented these concepts in terms of what they (the houses) were built of and how they (the Vikings) built them and thereafter posed no further problems. There was again a consensus that this box would probably be useful later and indeed proved to be so.

The group went through all the picture collections in each of the Country and Town House collections, some 20 plus in total. Each was a high quality colour photo presented as a full screen image (Fig. 3.3).

The importance of this last point, although not immediately of great significance, should not be underestimated. At a fundamental level it quite simply allowed all the children to see and touch it easily without creating any problems in seeing, taking turns or sharing. It also allowed everyone in the group to see it *at the same time* in a way that would have been difficult with a book. This meant that when one child pointed to something on the screen and made a point or asked a question about it *all* the rest of the group were able to be involved. (In terms of developing collaborative working, the suitability and accessibility of the materials used is perhaps an aspect that warrants further investigation.)

As the children moved, and just as easily moved back, through the pictures, they began to identify the ones that they thought would be most useful. In effect they were sorting and classifying with this first classification being complete houses rather than the pictures of roofs or walls or excavations. Each photo also had a few lines of descriptive text about the picture (Fig. 3.3). This has been kept to a minimum and the vocabulary has been thought about carefully with a child audience in mind, yet it avoids the fault of becoming either patronising or vague. The opportunity to have the text in large or standard text size is ever present and is another example of attention to the smaller details that are so important in helping realize grander aims.

A further, and more sophisticated, example of this is to be found where some words in this text were highlighted, some in bold, some underlined. The children didn't look for manuals, or use help balloons, they simply clicked on the word to see what happened. It was immediately apparent that a click on an underlined word gave rise to a map which showed where this place (the underlined words all being places) was on the map (Fig. 3.4), while a click on a word in bold gave an explanation of that word on the screen (in effect accessing a glossary). Of course atlases and dictionaries could have been used but if they had the whole flow and momentum of the investigation would

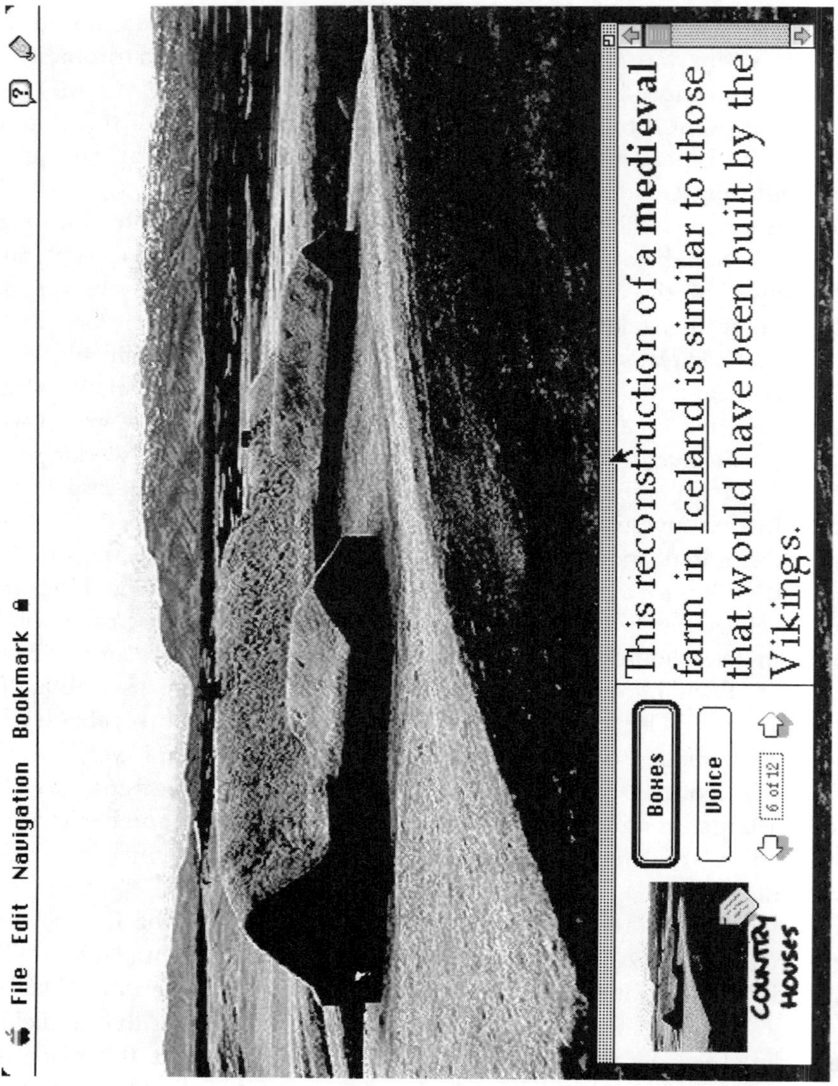
File Edit Navigation Bookmark
This reconstruction of a medieval farm in Iceland is similar to those that would have been built by the Vikings.
Boxes
Voice
6 of 12
COUNTRY HOUSES

Figure 3.3

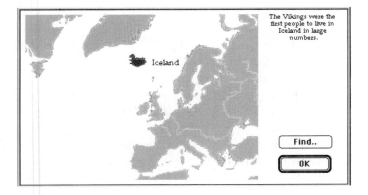

The Vikings were the
first people to live in
Iceland in large
numbers.

Iceland

Find..

OK

Figure 3.4

have interrupted for either some or all of the children in the group. Or, and I suggest this is more likely, neither the dictionaries nor the atlases would have been used, meaning that opportunities were missed and perhaps more seriously, concepts continued to be used by the program that the child or children didn't understand. The ease with which any member of the group could say 'What's that mean then?' when wattle and daub or turf or excavation was used in the text and get an immediate response led, I felt, to a greater willingness to be prepared to actually admit they didn't know or weren't sure. The glossary is quite comprehensive and the definitions given are not simplistic. As was shown by the group, children of this age would often struggle with some of these definitions but collectively, and at times with adult support, there were few that weren't within their grasp conceptually.

Returning to the group's task of finding out what Viking houses were like and 'How do we know that?', the first thing they did was to look at the complete houses pictures. This 'What did they look like?' and 'How do we know?' are considered separately here so that each can be explored in a little more depth. In effect, the two happened alongside each other, with one informing the other as the investigation proceeded.

Out of the twenty-odd pictures in the Town and Country Houses collections, the group found four complete house pictures, each with its own text. Unfortunately, they were not together in the sequence and trying to move between one and another to identify common features or differences proved too difficult and became very frustrating. The group clearly wanted to look at the house pictures they had identified as the most useful to their line of enquiry in quick succession or even better, alongside each other. But there were other factors now coming into play: the children were coming to the end of their concentration span, it was also coming up to playtime itself and it was PE afterwards! These are variables that cannot be denied in the primary classroom.

Skilful primary teachers have a range of strategies for putting on hold whatever the child or children are working on in a way that means it can be reactivated and continued at a later time.

In the example being considered here the IT component, and particularly the CD-ROM program facilitated this. *The World of the Vikings* has a Bookmark subtitle at the top of the screen throughout. Clicking on this produces a menu which includes 'mark picture', which enables the user to do this for all those pictures that are of particular interest for the current enquiry. These are then grouped together, in effect a sub-group on which the user can work without going through material already identified as superfluous. This is a powerful tool and was just what this group of children needed at this stage. However, this tool is made even more user-friendly by asking what the user wishes each saved picture to be known as. So, the 'straw house', 'the house on the hill', 'grass roof', 'the big house' (as in Fig. 3.3) were the names chosen by the children after some discussion. The group was given its own disk and these pictures were saved to it for future reference and, armed with their crisps and oranges, the group headed for the playground!

It was seen in the earlier part of this chapter how this teacher was particularly concerned to develop the 'how do we know that?, where's the evidence?' component of teaching history with children. It was also seen how the books and posters usually used to support children's studies on the Romans, Anglo-Saxons and Vikings were limited in this area. Where the evidence *was* presented, the style and language of the books almost always prevented the children being able to make good use of them.

Did the use of CD-ROMs make for progress in this area? Did it offer the children the opportunity to answer this 'How do we know that?, Where's the evidence?' in a way that was not possible using other media?

In the example used above based on *The World of the Vikings*, it was seen how the children focused on the pictures of complete houses rather than ones of doors, roofs or interiors. One of these was identical to the photo in one of the reference books brought together by the teacher to support this topic. This was immediately recognized by the children and the same questions arose. 'How do they know?' This is where the sheer storage power and speed of access to what is stored on the CD-ROM came into its own. It was noted above that the Bookmark option was ever present at the top of the screen and could be used to mark pictures that were of particular interest to a line of enquiry and to form a sub-group with these. Another option on the menu that drops down when Bookmark is clicked is one entitled About Picture. When this is selected details about the picture in use (that is on the screen) are

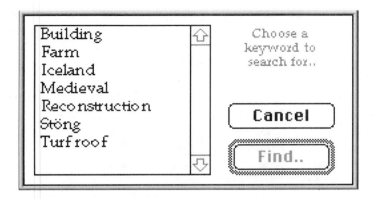

Figure 3.5

superimposed upon the picture. The information is not dense text but is rather a skeleton outline of known information about the picture including what it is, where it was found and where it is now and, of particular interest here, whether it is a reconstruction or not. This facility enabled the children to move into the 'how we know' for a historical period where it is virtually impossible to have access to primary source material and to do so with ever-increasing confidence. However, if it had stopped at this stage it would be useful but quite limited – but it doesn't. An option at the bottom of this About Picture information is Keywords and a click here presents another list of words to do with the picture (Fig. 3.5). A click on one of these which may be of interest, say 'building' or 'turf roof', brings in another collection of pictures related to the new concept: archaeologists at work, aerial views of Viking settlements, post holes and wicker work from Jorvik, and one can choose to explore these or go back. This is so important with the young learner as the need to go back to previous points is often felt. The 'go back' option is always available with this program and is found on most CD-ROMs and is a very necessary tool. To draw upon a classic historical image it is almost like rolling out a ball of wool behind you as you move off. This gives you the confidence to explore knowing that you can always find your way back to a previous point and eventually out again at any time!

In an early investigation into the use of CD-ROMs with children (NCET, 1994) there is a wonderful quote from one of the children that captures the difference between this medium and others used.

'A book has a front, a middle and an end – a CD-ROM goes round and round.'

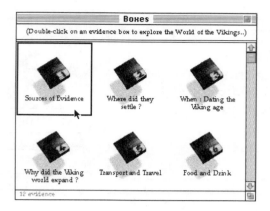

Figure 3.6

This same report also drew attention to the findings of one piece of research that strongly suggested that adult learners were less happy with this more open-ended walk through the available material, whereas children were quite at one with it. Teachers will have to be careful that they don't simply impose their own reference frameworks on the children they work with without realizing it. It *may* be that new ways of access to ever increasing amounts of information require us all to consider alternative ways of approaching it.

All historical investigations start with either a question, a series of questions, or with the posing of a hypothesis. However, this is not a linear process which one moves through from beginning to end. The answer to one question invariably gives rise to another, just as the examination of one piece of evidence causes a need to re-examine previous conclusions. And so it was with the children in this example. They had had initial questions to prompt the investigation and had used the CD-ROM to gain access to source material that was almost certainly not available to them, or indeed to almost anyone for that matter, in any other form and in such quality and quantity. They had been able to satisfy themselves that it was reliable, historically sound information because they had been able to examine where it had come from and how the interpretation given to it had been arrived at. It was very encouraging to note that there was increasing use made of the Sources of Evidence (Fig. 3.6) box of the Viking CD-ROM by this and other groups as the topic developed. The children's grasp of the main sources of primary evidence definitely moved forward during this topic and for several of the more able children so did their understanding of the potential strengths and weaknesses of these forms of evidence.

This small scale research project is ongoing and there are also whole areas of this particular CD-ROM that have not been commented on here. What was becoming apparent as this chapter was being written was the tremendous scope there was for differentiating the tasks presented to the children when they had access to the CD-ROM. The whole area of differentiation is returned to (below), but what was so encouraging in the above was that it was possible to differentiate the task by *the ability to understand the concepts*. This level of conceptual understanding does not run in parallel with either reading or writing ability, which is so often seen to lead any differentiation that takes place.

Developing an IT capability

The final chapter considers in greater depth the contributions made to each child's developing IT capability by being involved in activities like the above in his/her history topics. However, it is worth noting here just some features of the IT programme of study for this key stage that the above example touches upon:

> Pupils should be taught to extend the range of IT tools that they use for . . . investigation . . . become discerning in their use of IT: select information, sources and media for their suitability for purpose . . . .

Pupils should have opportunities to:

> use IT to explore and solve problems in the context of work across a variety of subjects;
>
> examine and discuss their experiences of IT, and assess its value in their working practices;
>
> investigate parallels with the use of IT in the wider world, consider the effects of such uses, and compare them with other methods;
>
> use IT equipment and software to organise, reorganise and analyse ideas and information;
>
> select suitable information and media, and classify and prepare information for processing with IT, checking for accuracy;
>
> interpret, analyse and check the plausibility of information held on IT systems, and select the elements required for particular purposes, considering the consequences of any errors. (IT, PoS, Key Stage 2; DFE, 1995)

It can be seen that creating situations whereby children will have opportunities to use IT in history-based topics, such as those considered above, can hardly fail to make a contribution to the development of this capability. What was noticeable in the examples used above was the children's willingness and confidence to explore the limitations of the software they were using. 'I wonder if it will . . .' or 'I wonder if it can do . . .' were phrases increasingly heard once the children's investigations were underway. The honest answer from the adults was usually 'I'm not sure let *us* see . . .' or 'Try it and let me know . . .'. As was explored in the opening chapter, and is returned to in the final one, the significance of the teacher and his/her response as these situations arise is of great importance.

Conclusion

In this classroom and in this topic the use of IT was just one part of a much larger and wider agenda. The details extracted from this in the previous pages are no more than snapshots from this broader canvas. The house group still had to use their increased knowledge of this particular aspect of Viking life to explore how it helped them better understand what this life was like during this period of time, how it was both similar and different, and why. The hypotheses on why the Vikings left their homelands and came to Britain remained to be answered. The impact they may have had on the people who lived there then and the long-term legacy through to the lives of the children involved in this investigation today were similar big questions that also remained.

As has been noted earlier, the intention of this book is to attempt to explore how the use of IT can often facilitate and sometimes enhance the realization of the aims for a history topic that would be undertaken anyway. In other words, the IT component could contribute to it being done better, that is, more successfully. However, it was also suggested that there may be times when the appropriate use of IT can take school history into areas and on to planes where it could quite simply not go otherwise.

The use of the CD-ROM in this topic on the Vikings is, I would wish to claim, an example of this third level. This is a large claim to make and it is not done lightly. The difficulty of giving the children access to otherwise unavailable and inaccessible source material is a major one in any topic likely to be undertaken in the primary classroom and teachers have shown themselves to be incredibly resourceful in recent years. Some of the collections of primary source material relating to the 1930s to the Present Day in terms of artefacts ranging through clothes to music to photographs (and much more) will be the envy of many a museum in years to come. Teachers have become aware of how such collections and children being able to work with them opens up the processes of historical enquiry to the children. They know that hypotheses are more likely to be posed and questions asked when the children have this access. The fact that the National Curriculum now requires children to have this access to the process of historical enquiry as well as its end products is merely an acknowledgement of that fact that history itself cannot take place without it.

If the access to the resources is not present the ability to ask appropriate questions and pose these hypotheses is drastically reduced. Without the questions to drive an enquiry there is very limited scope to identify and then use the skills of the historian. The absence of these two is likely to lead to history being presented to children either via the text/reference book or the teacher. In effect it is the products of someone else's enquiries that are usually presented without any awareness of how these products came to be arrived at being developed with the children. This is what HMI found (DES, 1989) in its report on history in the primary school during the previous decade. Not only were the skills of history not being developed, but neither was a sufficient knowledge base, with the ultimate loss being the understanding.

The claim being made here is that the arrival of CD-ROM technology in the primary school and the development of specific programs of the quality and appropriateness of *The World of the Vikings* is an example of IT doing rather more than facilitating and enhancing. The claim is that it makes it possible to take historical enquiry into areas which are not achievable by other means. The access to the source material, the opportunity to develop the necessary skills by working on it and the increase in the knowledge base cannot be separated in practice and the example above attempted to demonstrate this. Together, the development of the child's understanding of both the particular historical period and the wider contribution history makes to his/her understanding of the world they live in and his/her place in it is advanced.

Although CD-ROM has been around since the late 1980s it is only really since 1993 that it has made an impact outside quite a narrow base. The government's injection of over £7,000,000 to 'prime pump' this development in 1994 and 1995 and particularly the targeting of primary education for a large part of this money is very encouraging. The quality of many of the CD-ROM disks in the mid-1990s is very variable and many that are being offered to schools are quite simply unsuitable. Schools will have to think carefully about the criteria they wish to apply to inform their purchasing decisions to ensure they are choosing wisely. The National Council of Education Technology (NCET) will have an important role to play in this process and has already been involved in drawing up recommended disk lists. It is the home market that is obviously being targeted by the big software houses and schools will need to take care that the 'all-singing, all-dancing' disks (including video footage of famous films starring famous actors) are the ones that can be most useful in an educational context. I suggest that this is likely to often not be the case.

The brief and as-yet incomplete observations reported here of this group of

7- to 8-year-olds working with a well-constructed and appropriately designed CD-ROM give an insight into the contribution it can make to the learning situation. I suggest an encouraging insight because it definitely created a situation in which the children could use and further develop their historical skills and understanding. It created this situation in a topic on a historical period that has proved very difficult to achieve this using other resources. This meant that the process of history, the involving of the children in 'how we know', remained mainly inaccessible when compared to what has begun to be achieved in topics such as 1930s to the Present Day. The reasons why this is not only desirable but necessary to fulfil the National Curriculum requirements were explored earlier in the chapter.

The Pyramids, remains in Benin and the Indus valley and the Aztec cities have all been mentioned as being inaccessible in a similar way. With carefully constructed and produced CD-ROMs this inaccessibility for children studying them in their classrooms can almost certainly be reduced. To maximize the potential of this new medium takes one into a much broader agenda considering approaches to learning and teaching styles. These are returned to and considered further in the final chapter, but it is right to acknowledge them here, as creating the technology is merely the first step.

Making a personal aside here, I consider the recent development in CD-ROM technology to be one of the most exciting since the introduction of computers into schools in the early 1980s. I believe it offers significantly increased opportunities for children to organize and pursue their enquiries in a way that gives them increased control and therefore freedom with, and over, the material they work with than by almost any other means currently available.

In Papert's latest book (1993) he has a lovely example of Leonardo having the vision of aeroplanes and powered flight but it was not until the technology reached a further stage of development that it actually became possible to realize these ideas. He suggests that computers may be the technology to help realize the visions of the earlier progressive educators with their ideas of children as independent, autonomous learners. I would not claim *too* much for recent developments in the field of CD-ROMs, but it does seem to be a technological advance that certainly creates many new and as yet to be explored avenues. The implications for teachers, learning and the wider aspects of classroom life are very considerable. An attempt to explore these a little further is undertaken in the final chapter.

References

Bruner, J. (1963) *The Process of Education.* New York: Vintage Books.
Bruner, J. (1966) *Towards a Theory of Instruction.* New York: Harvard University Press.

Collingwood, R.G. (1946) *The Idea of History.* London: Clarendon Press.

DES (1989) *Aspects of Primary Practice: The Teaching and Learning of History and Geography.* London: HMSO.

DES (1991a) *History in the National Curriculum.* London: HMSO.

DES (1991b) *History Non-statutory Guidance.* London: HMSO.

DES (1991c) *Aspects of Primary Practice: The Teaching and Learning of Information Technology.* London: HMSO.

DFE (1995) *Key Stages 1 and 2 of the National Curriculum.* London: HMSO.

Garland, R. (ed.) (1982) *Microcomputers and Children in the Primary School.* Sussex: Falmer Press.

HMI (1989) *Standards in Education 1987: The Annual Report of the Senior Chief Inspector Based on the Work of HMI in England.* London: DES.

HMI (1990) *Standards in Education 1988–9: The Annual Report of the Senior Chief Inspector of Schools.* London: HMSO.

Kelly, A.V. (ed.) (1984) *Microcomputers and the Curriculum.* London: Harper & Row.

Lawlor, S. (1991) Interview on Channel 4 TV programme *Clean Slate,* 15 February.

Maddison, A. (1982) *Microcomputers in the Classroom.* London: Hodder & Stoughton.

Mortimore, P., Sammons, P., Stoll, L., Lew, D. and Ecob, R. (1989) *School Matters: The Junior Years.* Wells, Somerset: Open Books.

NCC/SEAC (1993a) *The National Curriculum and Its Assessment: An Interim Report by Sir Ron Dearing.* London: HMSO.

NCC/SEAC (1993b) *The National Curriculum and Its Assessment: Final Report.* London: HMSO.

NCET (1994) *CD-ROM in Education.* Coventry: NCET.

OFSTED (1993) *Curriculum Organisation and Classroom Practice in Primary Schools: A Follow-up Report.* London: OFSTED.

OFSTED (1994) *Primary Matters: A Discussion on Teaching and Learning in Primary Schools.* London: OFSTED.

OFSTED (1995) *The Annual Report of Her Majesty's Chief Inspector of Schools.* London: OFSTED.

Papert, S. (1980) *Mindstorms: Children, Computers and Powerful Ideas.* Hemel Hempstead, Herts: Harvester Press.

Papert, S. (1993) *The Children's Machine: Rethinking School in the Age of the Computer.* Hemel Hempstead, Herts: Harvester Press.

Parker, C. and Smart, L. (1992) *Making Links.* Coventry: NCET.

Past Forward (1993) *The World of the Vikings* (CD-ROM). York: Past Forward.

Rogers, P.J. (1987) *History: Why?, What? and How?* London: Historical Association.

Rosenthal, R. and Jacobson, L. (1968) *Pygmalion in the Classroom: Teacher Expectation and Pupils' Intellectual Development.* New York: Holt, Rinehart & Winston.

Schools Council (1978) *History 13–16.* Edinburgh: Holmes McDougall.

Schools Council (1980) *History, Geography and Social Studies (8–13): Place, Time and Society.* London: Collins.

Smart, L. and Taylor, D. (in press) The use of CD-ROMs in the development of historical understanding in the lower primary years.

CHAPTER 4

Life in Tudor Times

The Tudor period is one that has always seemed to capture the imagination. Larger-than-life characters, great deeds of daring, famous military events, fantastical fashions, wonderful achievements in the arts and sciences – and more. This colour and richness has provided the backdrop for numerous TV series, several Oscar-winning films and countless novels, and is' likely to continue to do so. The wider interest in this period of history has meant most people know something about it and of some of the characters who lived during it in a way that may not be matched by any other historical period in British history. There also appears to be a 'feel-good' factor associated with this period in many people's minds, which seems to include King Henry VIII and Queen Elizabeth I standing up to more powerful foreign enemies – and defeating them! It includes indomitable British seamen sailing to far-off exotic places, culminating with Drake sailing right around the world. The new foods, herbs and material riches brought back from these voyages only add to the magic. At home the arts flourished and this was the era of Shakespeare. Economically Britain moved from the rigid structures of the mediaeval period both on the land and in the world of commerce, with very significant impacts on the ownership of wealth and its knock-on effect into the field of political influence and power. One could continue.

All of the above, like all history, are interpretations of what we know of this period. Other interpretations have been made, and will continue to be made of the characters and events and of the significance of the Tudor period. However these events are interpreted one thing seems clear: it is not a period that can be ignored. It was not surprising, therefore, that it was included in the compulsory part of the history curriculum right from the first drafts from the original Working Group (DES, 1990) through to the revised Mark II model of 1995 (DFE, 1995). That is, the Tudor period survived the pruning of the National Curriculum Mark I and into the Mark II version of 1995, but it needs to be remembered that this study unit was Tudor and Stuart Times in the original statutory orders (DES, 1991a) and indeed for the first four years of the history National Curriculum.

It was seen earlier in the book how Key Stage 2 history suffered from chronic overload in terms of the content that had to be covered and how, eventually, this was acknowledged by Dearing in the revisions he advised to the government in late 1993 (NCC/SEAC, 1993b). The need to reduce the overall content of the curriculum was the reason why Tudor and Stuart Times became merely Tudor Times and it was an acknowledgement that it was not possible to do the Tudor and Stuart period in the half a term that most schools allocated to each of the required history topics.

From September 1995 primary schools will therefore be undertaking a topic based on Life in Tudor Times. As with topics based on Romans, Anglo-Saxons and Vikings, it will not be the content itself that is so different from similar topics that were undertaken prior to the introduction of the National Curriculum, but rather the way in which they are studied. The National Curriculum requirements have attempted to rectify some of the serious shortcomings that HMI had found in their report on history in the primary school (DES, 1989a). The framework for history teaching and learning created by the National Curriculum was one that attempted to establish a balance between the content to be studied and the manner in which it was to be studied; a balance between the 'what we know' and the 'how we know it'. Despite some attempts to re-open the debate about this 'balance' when the Dearing Review (NCC/SEAC, 1993a) was underway, this original model survived.

As was also seen in the previous two chapters, the broader historical concepts and skills and the understanding of the processes of history are detailed in the Key Elements section of the Statutory Orders and these are common to all the history undertaken at Key Stage 2. The content that is specific to each topic to be studied is detailed in the individual Study Units.

For the period that this chapter focuses on these are as follows. As the contribution of IT to the realization of these aims is considered in the main body of this chapter, constant reference will be made back to them

Study Unit: Life in Tudor Times

Pupils should be taught about some of the major events and personalities, including monarchs, and the way of life of people at different levels of society in Tudor times:

Major events and personalities
a. Henry VIII and the break with Rome, *e.g. the divorce question, the dissolution of the monasteries*
b. exploration overseas, *e.g. the voyages of Sebastian and John Cabot, Francis Drake and Walter Raleigh*
c. Elizabeth I and the Armada (1588).

The ways of life of people at different levels of society
d. Court life, *e.g. the progresses of Elizabeth I, the role of a personality such as Thomas More or the Earl of Essex*
e. ways of life in town and country, *e.g. home life, work and leisure, health, trade*
f. arts and architecture, including Shakespeare, *e.g. Elizabethan theatres, music, paintings, town houses, manor houses, and country houses and their estates.*

One can see that even with the removal of the Stuart period from this study unit there is still a lot of material to be covered. However, it is only when one adds the requirements contained in the Key Elements to the above that the whole picture is revealed.

Key Elements

The key elements outlined below are closely related and should be developed through the Study Units, as appropriate. Not all the Key Elements need to be developed in each Study Unit.

Pupils should be taught:

1. **Chronology**
   a. to place the events, people and changes in the periods studied within a chronological framework;
   b. to use dates and terms relating to the passing of time, including ancient, modern, BC, AD, century and decade, and terms that define different periods, *e.g. Tudor, Victorian.*

2. **Range and Depth of Historical Knowledge and Understanding**
   a. about characteristic features of particular periods and societies, including the ideas, beliefs and attitudes of people in the past, and the experiences of men and women; and about the social, cultural, religious and ethnic diversity of the societies studied;
   b. to describe and identify reasons for and results of historical events, situations, and changes in the periods studied;
   c. to describe and and make links between the main events, situations and changes both within and across periods.

3. **Interpretations of History**
   a. to identify and give reasons for different ways in which the past is represented and interpreted.

4. **Historical Enquiry**
   a. how to find out about aspects of the periods studied, from a range of resources of information, including documents and printed sources, arte-facts, pictures and photographs, music, and buildings and sites;
   b. to ask and answer questions, and to select and record information relevant to a topic.

5. **Organisation and Communication**
   a. to recall, select and organise historical information, including dates and terms;
   b. the terms necessary to describe the periods and topics studied, including court, monarch, parliament, nation, civilisations, invasion, conquest, settlement, conversion, slavery, trade, industry, law;
   c. to communicate their knowledge and understanding of history in a variety of ways, including structured narratives and descriptions.
   (History, Programme of Study, Key Stage 2; DFE, 1995)

As was discussed in Chapter 1, the intention of this book is to consider how the use of IT can, if used appropriately, often facilitate and enhance the historical studies children are engaged in, and would be engaged in if IT was not used. The much larger claim, namely that there are times when the use of IT can take these studies on to a higher plane or into areas that are not achievable by other methods, has been made in previous chapters and will also be considered here.

This chapter focuses on the concept of chronology. This is not an everyday concept but it is a very important one for history. Its importance is now widely accepted in the teaching of school history in Britain (DES, 1985, 1986, 1989a, 1991a; DFE, 1995) but is not without challenge (Lello, 1980). Throughout the 1960s and 1970s a series of research projects explored children's under-standing of the concept of *time* in history (Jahoda, 1963; Hallam, 1967; Peel, 1967; Smith and Tomlinson, 1977). These were heavily influenced by the work of Jean Piaget and the Piagetian theory of learning. However, it was time that was central to these investigations and that is not the same as chronology, although the two are closely related. Despite the fact that chronology is widely used in official publications and guidance on school history, it is not easy to find a definition and I suggest the following as a working definition.

> Chronology is the sequencing of events/people/developments in relation to each other and to existing knowledge of other, already known, events/people/developments.

Sequence is the key word here, with its own meaning of 'putting in order', with some things being before and some coming after.

Each and every person has a chronological framework which is far wider than the study of history. Concepts such as before, after, a long time ago, tomorrow, last year, when I was younger, are all part of everyday vocabulary and it is difficult to have a conversation anywhere without the necessity to relate one event to another arising! For example, on the train: 'As I said to her yesterday . . .' and in the classroom: 'Now before playtime begins I just want to talk to you about that letter you took home to your parents yesterday . . .', etc.

Children develop a chronological framework very early in life and certainly before they arrive at school for the first time. Conversations involving phrases such as 'after breakfast', 'your sister will be home soon', 'before you go to bed', 'tomorrow' are commonplace in every home all around the country. All these phrases help the growing child to make sense, and then better sense of his/her world and his/her place in it. The chronological framework, the sequencing of events in relation to each other is constantly developing and increasing in sophistication – but each and every child has one and this needs to acknowledged by teachers, especially when they are teaching history.

The research referred to above focused on time rather than chronology and the former, being one of mathematics' key concepts, involves numbers. The following have been taken from popular school history books:

500 hundred years ago
Elizabeth I was queen for 45 years
1000 years before the Romans came to Britain the Egyptians . . .

and there was no difficulty in finding these or similar examples. There is no disputing that these large units of time are difficult to grasp, even more so if you have only lived some eight or nine years yourself! The research findings above led to some quite pessimistic conclusions as to what might be achieved with children in history in the primary school (i.e. Peel, 1967).

However, two factors have led to this position being reversed to such an extent that the youngest children in schools are now confidently expected to work with chronological frameworks when studying the past.

Probably the most significant of these was the further development in our understanding of the factors that affect children's learning. The increasing awareness of the importance of a meaningful context, of the social dimension of learning and of the part played by the teacher/adult have all contributed to this understanding. The development of Piaget's fundamental model by Donaldson (1978), the increasing influence of Bruner (1963, 1966, 1983, 1986) and Vygotsky (1962), and especially the importance attached to language (Vygotsky, 1962; Wells, 1987) are all key influences here. The impact of these influences on what can be expected of children in history continues to be felt.

The second factor has been the steady movement towards some form of consensus that the concept of time is not as important as an understanding of chronology in developing children's knowledge, skills and understanding in this curriculum area. Despite the fierce debates about this as the National Curriculum requirements were drawn up in the late 1980s the model that evolved was one that reflected this. The development of the child's chronological framework is now viewed as being more significant than the ability to know dates and time periods. There is, of course, no suggestion here that the former excludes the latter, and it will be suggested that the learner's ability to grasp the concept of time and particularly dates and period duration is developed *through* or more accurately *within* a chronological framework. I deliberately use 'learner' rather than 'child' here for I suggest this applies to all students of history.

However, while research into children's understanding of the actual concept of time is likely to continue, it is now accepted that children, from their earliest days in school, are capable of creating chronological frameworks. The work of John West in the late 1970s and early 1980s (West, 1978, 1981) was of great significance and made a major contribution to the way in which chronology and time are now handled in the primary classroom. West's work showed how primary aged children were quite competent at sequencing pictures and artefacts by using the evidence available from the picture/ artefact itself and the knowledge, information and understanding they brought to the task. Having undertaken similar activities with undergraduate and post-graduate student teachers on many occasions in recent years, it is quite clear that this interaction between the new information and the existing schemata is identical. One might anticipate that what the older learner brings to the situation is broader and of greater sophistication but this is often not the case! The value and use of toys as evidence has become increasingly realized in recent years, but anyone who has used them will almost certainly have had a few surprises. For most adults the subtleties of Barbie's joints, or the modifications made to He-Man's or the Power Ranger's armour in recent years, or whether Mega Drives came before Master Systems, can easily be overlooked or considered unimportant when seeking clues to place these items in a chronological order to relate them to other aspects of life. For a youngster living in the mid-1990s such unawareness almost defies belief. It is also very humbling. The skills being exercised by the children are parallel to those exercised by the experienced archaeologist who sequences the variety of coins unearthed on a dig. It is the skills of the historian that are being employed here and once again the early work of Bruner (1966) comes to mind. But, like the archaeologist, the child is often part of a group working on the task and the social interaction via the discussions and the pooling of 'the second record', that experience that each individual brings to the event, is likely to lead to a more comprehensive picture.

As already noted, the 1960s research into children's ability to work with the concept of time in history led to a quite pessimistic attitude to the teaching of this subject in the primary school, but by the early 1980s the shift of emphasis from time to chronology had brought about a very significant change of attitude. The HMI report of 1985 *History in the Primary and Secondary Years* acknowledged these developments and, importantly, gave its approval,

> The question of children's sense of time worries many teachers who see it as a stumbling block in the development of historical understanding. However, the ability to conceive of the duration of historical time and of the difference, for example, between 500 years and 2000 years is difficult not only for the young but for most adults too. It may be more helpful to concentrate less on historical time and more on an understanding of historical chronology, which is perhaps easier to identify and capable of being acquired by young children. *It provides a structure that enables children to make sense of what might otherwise be a kaleidoscope of events* [emphasis] (DES, 1985)

Not surprisingly the politicians responsible for the introduction of the National Curriculum were very keen that it be viewed as a major advance in the development of the educational system in this country. One of the ways adopted to create this perception was to present it as a *remedy* for the *deficiencies* of what had gone before – it was to be a fresh start. However, education development in Britain has been an evolutionary rather than a revolutionary process, and despite the rhetoric the National Curriculum can be seen to be very much part of this development. Indeed, it would be possible to make a case that it was in those areas where the National Curriculum moved too far from this evolutionary development that it failed and had to be revised.

The individual National Curriculum orders for each of the subject areas were very much part of this evolutionary development in their own fields. This can be clearly seen in the English and science orders and also in those that were issued for history, particularly with respect to the developments with regard to time and chronology, as outlined above.

Chronology features very prominently in the statutory requirements for each of the key stages. In Key Stage 2 it is the first of the Key Elements, which it will be remembered are common to all the topics and periods that are required to be studied. It reads

Pupils should be taught

1. **Chronology**
   a. to place the events, people and changes in the periods studied within a chronological framework;
   b. to use dates and terms relating to the passing of time, including ancient, modern, BC, AD, century and decade, and terms that define different periods, *e.g. Tudor, Victorian.*

In the wake of the work of West and its support by HMI (DES, 1985, 1989a), the use of timelines became an increasingly common feature in the primary classroom when a history-based topic was undertaken. The above section of the National Curriculum requirements has given timelines an added impetus. It can be seen how it is envisaged that the 'chronological framework' (**a** above) is intended to be developed further to 'use dates and terms relating to the passing of time' (**b** above).

Despite the name, it is 'chronology' and 'sequence' as opposed to specific units of time that timelines usually concern themselves with. They take on many forms, often drawn on notice boards, some using different length skipping ropes, others following the picture rail around the room and, sometimes, utilizing a washing-line and clothes-pegs. Once in place the teacher and the children add a wide range of materials to the line – photos, artefacts, drawings and clothes being some of the most commonly found; Cooper (1992) and Blyth

(1990) have some interesting and varied ideas and examples from work they have been involved in. What all the different variations and forms do is to create a *tangible* framework in which events, people and other elements can be *related* to each other and to existing knowledge. Using the earlier definition:

> Chronology is the sequencing of events/people/developments in relation to each other and to existing knowledge of other, already known, events/people/developments.

It can be visualized how a skipping rope representing grandpa's life might have a photo of an early motor car, a postage stamp of George VI, an old metal toy, a coin, etc., added to it, after discussion, at appropriate places. The timeline enables all these features to be be related and invariably leads to the questions that take the process of the investigation further by then giving rise to more questions. Why did that happen then? How did that invention affect the person's life? Did grandpa have a car, telephone, TV or whatever – if not why not? Why don't we have coins like that now? How many of these coins would you need to buy that toy?, etc. The pairs of concepts, continuity and change, similarity and difference and cause and effect considered in an earlier chapter and central to the process of historical enquiry are actively brought into play via the timeline. This point will be returned to later in the chapter.

For the teacher considering making use of a timeline to support the development of a sense of chronology with the children they work with, one particular feature is worth anticipating at the outset. It is likely that the original collection of artefacts, photos, etc., will be supplemented as the topic develops. This will mean that rearrangements of the existing materials will need to be made and it will almost certainly be necessary to move some items closer together. In other words it will be necessary to *play with time*. If the timeline takes the form of things stapled to walls this rearranging can be very difficult and it is suggested that the washing-line and pegs offer the greatest flexibility here. It will probably have been realized by this stage that it is not just the actual sequence along a line that is of importance but also the *gaps* between the things on the line – it is these gaps that represent time. It is through observing and discussing these gaps that will enable children to develop a greater level of sophistication in their use of the necessary terms: 'before', becoming 'a long time before'; 'after' becoming 'just after' and eventually this will help take them into using more precise units of measurement of time itself – i.e. year, decade, century. The parallels with the movement from non-standard units to standard units of measurement when the children are working with mathematics will probably not have escaped the reader. It is with this transition from the sequencing and 'non-standard units' to the use of, and subsequent development of a greater understanding of, concepts of time that IT can make a contribution.

Timelines and Tudors

In the previous two chapters it was argued that IT had to fit into topics and schemes of work that would have been undertaken anyway if it was to make a real contribution. In Chapter 1 the necessary conditions for successful innovation were considered and the requirement that it could be related to existing practice was one of the most important ones identified and this is acknowledged again here.

The following attempts to explore how the use of a computer timeline program can contribute to the issues discussed above in a way that takes the progress made throughout the 1980s in this important area of history a step further.

All teachers operating in the maintained sector will take the statutory orders as their guide when planning a topic on the Tudor period. Earlier it was seen how the Key Elements reflect and consolidate the developments in history teaching of the 1980s with its requirement that children develop their chronological framework in an increasingly sophisticated manner.

For most primary teachers this will take the form of, firstly, creating a situation whereby the children can relate the Tudors to their *existing* overall chronological framework, that is in relation to other periods or events that the children have studied or are aware of.

Secondly, most teachers will aim to create learning situations whereby the children are able to develop a grasp of the chronology *within* the period being studied, in this case the Tudors.

This awareness of the *sequence* of events is crucial in seeking to understand why they took the form they did, and nowhere is this more true than within this particular historical period.

The History Working Group's concept of history that, despite all the changes, survives to provide the model for school's history was quite clear on this:

> a grasp of that sequence (of events) is fundamental to an understanding of the relationship between events, and such concepts as cause and change. *Chronology therefore provides a mental framework or map* which gives significance and coherence to the study of history. [my emphasis] (History 5–16; DES, 1990)

So initially the challenge is to create a situation whereby the new topic is related to the existing chronological framework that the children bring. It could be done like this:

> The Tudor period began about 500 years ago and ended about 400 years ago. It lasted over 100 years. The Tudors came about 500 years after the battle of Hastings that we looked at last term and over 1500 years after the Romans first came to Britain, as you will know from last year's topic . . . .

The level of abstraction, the heavy presence of massive blocks of time and the lack of tangible reference points are likely to lead to confusion for at least some, if not most, of the children, and such an approach is unlikely to be adopted by a good primary school teacher.

It is suggested that the use of the timeline at the introductory stages of a new historical topic offers the teacher many advantages. A washing-line strung across the classroom and a collection of pictures such as those referred to below is likely to lead to a sounder grasp of just where and when the Tudor period fits into the children's existing chronological framework. I would suggest that all timelines/time frameworks need a reference point that the user is comfortable with and poses no conceptual problems. Probably the easiest one is 'now' and it is suggested that this is the most appropriate one for use with primary aged children. A photo of the class taken there and then, using a Polaroid-type camera, or today's newspaper or similar 'now' artefact, serves this purpose. It is then a question of what other pictures are used to identify periods, people and events prior to this and into which the Tudor period can eventually be introduced. (Of course it does not have to be pictures but a whole class session is envisaged here and the advantages of the picture over text or artefact is that it can quite simply be easier to display at a height which can be seen and therefore responded to, by all.) This choice of pictures will need to be made by each teacher in relation to his/her knowledge of the class, its interests, places visited on a school journey, characters recently referred to in assembly, previous topics undertaken, etc. They might include pictures of last year's class photo, the teacher as a child of their age, the opening of the Channel Tunnel, William the Conqueror, the Pyramids, Julius Caesar, Boudicca, Mary Seacole, the *Rocket*, King Asoka, the *Mary Rose*, Tyrannosaurus Rex, the opening of the school, etc. The possibilities are literally endless, but the key factor influencing the selection must be that they are *meaningful* to the children in that particular class. Perhaps eight or so pictures is about right for a normal-width classroom, so that reasonable-sized gaps can be left between the pictures. The reason for this is developed below.

Once the 'now' point has been established on the line the other pictures can be added one at a time, and it is suggested not in historical order. The way the children are organized to respond to each picture being added to the line could obviously vary, whole class, group or pairs, but it is the discussion that takes place prior to the placing of the picture on the line that is so important. 'Before' and 'after' will be key words but will almost certainly become qualified with 'just', 'soon', 'a long time'.

As more pictures are added (and it is important not to overcrowd the line, otherwise the gaps between the pictures cease to be of use), the advantages of the washing-line and clothes-pegs over the pinboard and staple gun come into play. Questions will almost certainly arise as to 'whether that gap is big enough' because the gaps will be seen to represent time, albeit in non-standard units. It is not impossible to imagine a comment along the lines of:

> The gap between when Miss was born and the opening of the Channel Tunnel needs to be smaller because it's the same as the dinosaurs to Julius Caesar and I think that was a lot longer. . . .

Having been involved in such activities with my own classes and observed other teachers undertaking similar tasks I continue to be surprised, and delighted, by the way the children become so involved and of the quality of the discussions that arise.

Eventually, a timeline with pictures and gaps emerges which provides, along with the previous discussions, an insight into the existing shared chronological framework of the children in a class. It is acknowledged of course that different levels of sophistication will remain but a shared framework to which all can relate is the aim here.

The Tudor period now needs to be added to this timeline. Again it can be done in a variety of ways, but where to locate it is likely to involve further discussion between the teacher and the class involving 'before' and 'after' vocabulary. Such a discussion usually provides some interesting insights into the children's starting points in relation to the topic being commenced. For identifying this period I used two lengths of coloured wool or ribbon that could be tied to the line and hung down marking, *in relation to the other events on the line*, just where the Tudor period occurred.

If successful, the period to be studied has now been identified and located within the chronological framework the class had created.

At the outset of this section it was suggested that most teachers would seek to do some form of 'location in time' activity at the *outset* of such a topic.

The development of this, the second stage, involves the chronology of events and people *within* the period being studied and is likely to be an *ongoing* process throughout the topic itself. It is here that IT can make a contribution that, it is suggested, both facilitates and enhances what might be achieved using other forms of timelines, such as the one discussed above.

CHRONOLOGY, TIMELINES AND IT

There are several computer timeline programs available and at least one for all the major makes of computers found in schools. They are all in effect sophisticated databases which have been designed to enable the data stored to be presented in a certain way – the timeline format. It is not the purpose of this book to evaluate specific programs and the reader is referred to the professional journals for detailed reviews and comparisons, although there is nothing to beat the offer of an approval period if and when a purchase is considered.

All the timeline programs have certain common features that can be quickly listed here before considering how they might contribute to the development of the children's knowledge, skills and understanding in a history topic on Life in Tudor Times.

All the programs now available have a scrolling screen display. If one thinks of this literally as a scroll, that is, as a continuous roll of paper held between two rollers of which a section can be seen at any time, one has the idea. Some programs have this scrolling movement from left to right across the screen (e.g. Bartholomew and Ramsey, 1990) and some from top to bottom (e.g. ESM, 1991). A case can be made for each one, but I have not seen either cause any difficulties for children.

All the programs have the facility to enter information on to the timeline. Some make use of symbols (i.e. a crown for a monarch, crossed swords for a battle) and some use text. All have the facility for the teacher and the children to enter their own information and for this to be presented on the timeline itself.

All are designed so that when this item on the timeline is chosen it opens a page on which more detailed information can be written or read. Increasingly there is the facility to add pictures to this page as well, but reservations must be expressed about the usefulness of these in the form currently available.

A further significant feature the programs share is the ability to relate events to each other. This is done by having one set of events above (or to the left of) the timeline in the middle of the screen and another set below (or to the right of) the line itself. An example within the Tudor topic being considered here would be to have the reigns of the Tudor monarchs on one side of the line and important voyages of exploration on the other. This feature can be seen in Figure 4.1.

As was discussed earlier in this chapter this ability to 'relate' events is a key part of developing historical understanding and will be considered in more depth below.

All the programs enable the user to print out the timeline itself or sections of it at any time. The importance of this simple and now widely expected feature should not be underestimated as it allows what is happening with the computer to be *integrated* into the broad range of classroom activities that make up the topic.

These then are the key features of the main timeline computer programs available. There are many more sophisticated features that have not been mentioned here, but they are really embellishments on the basic model outlined above.

How then might programs like these be used to support the topics on

Tudor Life that will take place in the 20,000 or so primary schools across the country every year? What can they offer to contribute that other methods can or cannot do as well?

Consider first the National Curriculum requirement that all the above schools will have as one of their aims for this Tudor Life topic:

Pupils should be taught to place the events, people and changes in the periods studied within a chronological framework. (Key Elements, KS2; DFE, 1995)

and

Pupils should be taught about some of the major events and personalities, including monarchs. . . . [The latter to include Henry VIII and break with Rome, exploration overseas, Elizabeth and the Armada.]
(Study Unit Tudor Life; DFE, 1995)

Some form of framework must be set up and the timeline is the ideal medium here. The washing-line or around the wall variety of the earlier example could certainly be used and I have used this myself. Initially there are no problems, but as more and more events and people are added to it, it becomes overfull. One of the first losses when this happens is the gaps, as things are required to be moved closer together because of the pressures of space. The other difficulty is conveying *duration* of time on the line. The reigns of the Tudor monarchs have traditionally been used by many teachers to work their way through this century and, although there are several alternative approaches, this is likely to remain popular. There is therefore the need to indicate on the timeline when the Henrys were on the throne, when Mary reigned, etc. Different coloured paper on the wall or coloured ribbon on the washing-line are just two methods I have seen recently, and if it were only the monarchs' reigns that involved duration of time as opposed to one-off events (i.e. the Armada), clarity might be maintained. But what about Shakespeare and Thomas More or the dissolution of the monasteries? These were people or events that also require more than one-off entries on the timeline. What seems to happen is that either the timeline becomes so overcrowded that its usefulness to the children as a way of representing the sequence of people and events for ease of reference decreases very dramatically or, to maintain the clarity, only some events are entered. Where the latter occurs it tends to be the kings and queens and the rich and famous who are included and the ongoing events that are left off. Clarity is maintained but at a cost to the children's perceptions as to what and who was important and by default what and who wasn't.

It is suggested that the use of a computer timeline program may enable the clarity to be maintained, even when the amount and variety of information is large. Later, it will be explored how this *organizational* feature creates greater *learning* opportunities for the children to ask questions and pose hypotheses relating to this data. It is important to remember that it is not being collected and organized for its own sake.

It is not uncommon for a teacher undertaking a topic on Life in Tudor Times to organize the children into groups to work on different aspects of life during the period. A clear operating framework is necessary to prevent such degenerating into the dreaded copying of drawings and slightly modified text that has often been used to present topic work in a negative light (OFSTED, 1993a). However, using the pairs of concepts referred to throughout this book – continuity and change, similarity and difference and cause and effect – can provide a sound basis for the children's investigations. If each group uses a Key Question approach: 'who', 'what', 'when', 'where', 'why', and the ever present 'how do we know?' to organize its tasks, there should be no danger of the former happening. What focus each group might be given will obviously vary but using the National Curriculum guidelines might well include groups investigating some of the following – monarchs, exploration, leisure, religion, country life, town life, transport or houses. This list is neither exclusive nor is it recommended, it simply calls upon the observations made as to the way many teachers approach this topic.

Implicit in this approach of different groups exploring in depth their particular area is the assumption that at some stage during the topic they will organize and communicate their findings to the the rest of the class. The National Curriculum model of history recognizes that these two, organization and communication, are vital to each child's development in this discipline.

Pupils should be taught:

to . . . select and organise historical information . . .
to communicate their knowledge and understanding of history in a variety of ways.
(Key Elements, KS2; DFE, 1995)

The following is a series of suggestions as to how a computer timeline program might be used in a situation such as the one above. The potential benefits of doing so are then considered.

It needs to be stated that the computer is here seen as just one tool (and later a resource) among many that the children will use during a topic like this. Some of the others would almost certainly include a range of books, TV/radio/video programmes, a visit to a Tudor house/street or a museum with relevant displays, use of artefacts or portraits from the period (both of these being likely to be replicas), some period music, maybe some drama, certainly some art and or/design technology activities. It is suggested that IT's place is quite simply alongside these other tools and resources used to help develop the desired knowledge and understanding of this period of history.

Each group would be given a disk with a copy of the timeline program for its own use on its area of enquiry. All new computer programs require a familiarization period for the user, whether they are being used by children or adults. This is explored in more detail in the chapter on 'Classroom Considerations', where one of the points made is that a sense of purpose needs to be established for this getting to know the program to be successful. It is suggested here that each group enters on to its own blank timeline the dates of succession of each of the Tudor monarchs. Later in this chapter it will be seen how these individual databases will be merged, but this simple first stage achieves two key things. Firstly, it creates a situation whereby the children take ownership of the program by entering their data and at the same time develop the basic skill of using the program with success. Secondly, each group has created parallel structures for entering their specific data and as their investigations develop this will enable dialogue between the groups to be easier. At the later merging (putting all together) of the different groups' timelines, this structure will be a further advantage. Such a monarch-based structure is not a reflection of the writer's royalist sympathies or otherwise; the framework could easily be decade by decade or a series of other events, but it is suggested that some form of basic and shared framework is created in the early stages.

Each group, guided by the paired concepts and key questions outlined above (or some other set of guidelines drawn up with the teacher) commences its investigations. There is no one way this should be done but the *need* to record some of the information uncovered will soon become apparent. Historical investigation is not a linear process where one seeks out the information then asks questions of it – the two are interwoven at virtually every stage. If one focuses on the group of children investigating Exploration to see what might occur, it is possible to see how the computer-based timeline program can begin to play its part.

The Cabot brothers, Drake and Raleigh are the only named explorers in the National Curriculum (and these as examples only) but they provide a starting-point. As the children use their Key Questions to develop their enquiries, 'Where did he go?', 'When did he go?', 'Why did he go?', 'How do we know?', 'Who did he take with him?', etc. they will soon become aware that each of these does not simply make one voyage but several. Different years, different destinations, different reasons for making the voyage and different degrees of success will soon become apparent. This is a lot of information and particularly a lot of variables to hold. Children have traditionally kept their work in books and folders and with these investigations it might take the form of a page or even short chapter on each of the explorers they were asked to investigate. Sketches of the ships, maps of the routes, lists of the crew and life on board ship featuring alongside notes made from reference books, CD-ROM resource disks, videos watched and possibly a visit, all contribute to the building up of a picture of what was involved in ventures such as these. What is more difficult and I suggest not done so often is to *relate* these different individual voyages of discovery to each other and then place them in the context of the wider developments happening in the period itself. Yet it is only if this is attempted that we can seek to help to make sense of the individual bits of information they have often so diligently researched and presented. Without this the children are likely to end up with only 'the kaleidoscope of events' that HMI warned teachers of (DES, 1985).

It is the way this *knowledge* is used that will contribute to that wider goal of developing a greater *understanding*. It is important to remind ourselves occasionally that it is the latter we are seeking and must keep in sight; the knowledge that Cabot or Drake sailed to x and y, in itself, is useful when playing Trivial Pursuits, but history must be about moving beyond bits of knowledge and into *relating* them to develop and deepen our understanding of life in other times. This search for understanding involves addressing the three pairs of concepts mentioned earlier: similarity and difference, continuity and change and cause and effect. To be able to move into the areas covered by these concepts it is necessary to be able to compare and contrast what has been found out, to be able to relate things to each other both within and across the period of a particular topic.

If this Exploration group enters its findings on one of the computer-based timeline programs of the sort detailed above, the ability to relate, to compare and contrast, is placed at their disposal in a way that is very difficult if not impossible by other means. Such a claim needs to be substantiated and the following uses actual screen shots from a timeline program to attempt to do this. What is obviously not possible on these pages is to be able to scroll to see what information comes before and what after that which is actually on the screen at the moment. The reader will have to take on trust that this is there and what appears on this page is merely a section (one computer screen's worth) of this larger amount of information.

As with all the groups of children exploring different aspects of Tudor life, this group has its own disk. On this it has already entered the Tudor monarchs' dates of succession, which all the groups entered early in the topic. Using reference books and information from other sources they decide to begin their enquiries with the who, the where and the when questions. Literally who sailed where and in what year? Initially they focus on the named explorers of the National Curriculum, Drake, Raleigh and the Cabots. However, one of the major and ongoing criticisms of the National Curriculum for history is that it is too Anglo-centric. The problems caused by such an approach are clearly seen in the Tudor life study unit when one is looking at something like exploration. If only the above English (or employed by the English) explorers are considered, not only is their contribution distorted but it

91

actually works against the development of an understanding of the significance of the contribution they made. Significance in history is always debatable but few would argue that this wider exploratory movement, the Age of Exploration, was of great significance in bringing all parts of the world into contact with each other in a way that had never previously happened. As a great deal of this happened during the Tudor period in England the wider and the national scenes must be *related* in any attempt to understand them. For this reason the children also had the names of Columbus, Cortes, Cartier, Fernandez, da Gama, Magellan, Pizarro and Vespucci added to their list of explorers to answer these basic who, where and when questions. Not all would need to be investigated in depth, but to be able to see how Cabot, Raleigh and Drake's voyages were related chronologically to those of Columbus, da Gama and Magellan and others could only be beneficial to the children's understanding. As they began to examine the similarities and differences between the different voyages it became clear that it was not just the British who were interested in exploration at this time. And this is confining oneself to the area of exploration and discovery: an attempt to understand the Armada at a later stage in the topic would be very difficult without this awareness of the overlapping explorations.

However, before moving on to consider the wider benefits in terms of historical understanding that might arise from an awareness of the chronology of events, it is useful to examine how the above data might look on a computer timeline. Figure 4.1 shows what the timeline would look like once the children had researched and put on some of the European explorers' voyages (Fig. 4.1).

The children would obviously be involved in deciding what heading/phrase might be entered on the timeline to convey the most important bit of the information they had gathered about a person or a particular voyage (Fig. 4.1). The ability to be able to do this is a skill useful far beyond the immediate purposes here. There is a considerable amount of useful information that has already been gathered here in terms of establishing the basic chronological framework for looking at voyages of discovery during this time. One of the delights of working with children on tasks like this is that one simply never knows what observations or comments will be made in relation to the data they have collected, but each is likely to lead to further discussion – not just any discussion either but a historically based discussion in which comments will have to be supported with reference to the available evidence, in which observations will have to be qualified with 'as far as we know' and in which more questions than answers are likely to arise.

If the timeline program only allowed this one line of text entry it would be of very limited value, but it doesn't. Once the one-line summary or title has been entered on the line, a click with the mouse followed by a click on the

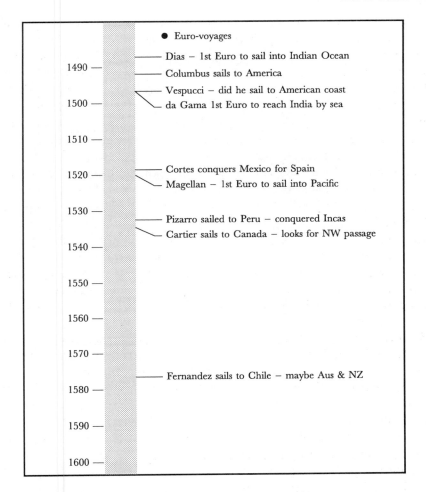

Figure 4.1

appropriate icon (small picture presenting words) will present the user with a whole screen on which further text can be added. These are usually referred to as record cards, and if the traditional card index filing system comes to mind, that is appropriate. On these the children can type in further information. They could use the Key Questions leading their investigations as subheadings if they wish. Although I have not seen it done in a classroom yet, what they can also do is leave their own thoughts or questions not answered so far on the cards as well. Indeed, if the teacher encourages the final heading to be 'Thoughts so far' or 'Next we need to know' or something similar, the group will be prompted to discuss and agree some statement here. Figure 4.2 is a hypothetical but, I suggest, not an unrealistic entry.

Drake sails around the world

1577 AD–1580 AD

Francis Drake left England in 1577. Queen Elizabeth 1st had told him to go and explore to see if he could find a way to India by sailing westwards. He also had permission to attack the Spanish and capture any treasure he could. Everyone wanted to find this route which they thought would be quicker. He had 3 ships with him and about 160 sailors. His ship was called the Golden Hind.

THOUGHTS: We wonder if he meant to sail around the world, we don't think he did. Were his sailors scared of

Page 1

Drake sails around the world

1577 AD–1580 AD

falling off the edge of the world if they thought it was flat? Can we find this out? Are there any sailors' diaries or ships' log books or did Elizabeth give him the orders to go right round?

TO DO: Draw a map of his route marking on all the countries he stopped at.

Page 2

Figure 4.2

At this stage the main contribution the computer timeline is providing is support for the *collating* and *recording* of information uncovered in a manner which is *systematic* and easily *accessible*. As was identified above, the collection and collation of data and the asking of questions of it is not a linear process and the facility to leave one's questions with the data and to be able to return to it later is a very powerful one. Too often in the classroom the questions that we all recognize as central to the development of a child's understanding seem to arise at awkward times (i.e. end of the lesson, conversation in the queue for the dining hall, etc.) and evaporate before they can be used to move that understanding forward. This is not unique to either children or classroom life, of course; as adults we may scribble a note in a margin or diary or attach a 'post-it' about issues or questions we intend to return to.

What we have then is a situation where the computer is once again acting as a support for learning. Bruner's concept of 'scaffolding' (Wood *et al.*, 1976) as discussed in the previous chapter, immediately springs to mind as the children are offered support in the development of the key skill being sought here; the skill of being able to organize the available information in such a way as to provide insights (or tentative answers) into the enquiry being undertaken. In the context of the Exploration group it would allow them to begin to answer the questions they had identified at the outset of its enquiry: who went where and when. The interwoven nature of the gathering of this information in relation to the initial questions posed and the natural way it prompts further questions and hypotheses was touched upon above. Skilful teaching involves being able to encourage the children to reflect upon what they have achieved and help them to identify the next step. This is certainly so in the history topic under consideration here.

The way the computer timeline enables the data already collected by this group to be presented back to them makes this reflecting on what has been achieved so far and the identification of the next question or hypothesis easier to achieve.

Figure 4.3 begins to really illustrate just how the use of IT in this context can make a significant contribution to not just facilitating but actually promoting this. In this printout it can be seen how two sets of data have been brought together. On one side of the line is the information gathered about the required English explorers and on the other side are the main voyages of the explorers from other countries. The left-hand margin puts these in the context of the Tudor period.

Again it is impossible to be sure what observations and questions might arise from the children being able to re-examine and reflect upon the information collected. However, the *relating* of one event to another or one event to all or some of the others is likely to inform these. The ability to *compare and contrast* – who went where, who was being sponsored by which head of which country, the intended destinations of the voyages, the lengths of the voyages, the reasons for the voyages, the success or failure of the voyages, the actual sequence of the voyages and more – is certainly facilitated for the children with this use of IT.

The paired concepts of similarity and difference, of continuity and change

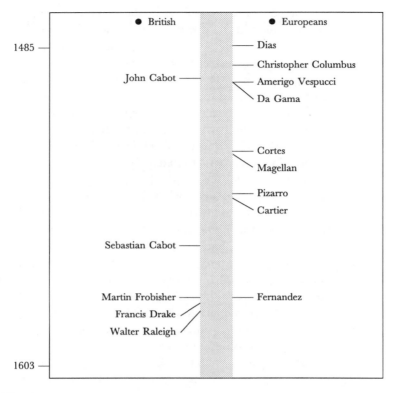

Figure 4.3

and maybe insights into cause and effect that were earlier identified as being central to the process of historical enquiry, and thus the discipline itself, would all come into play here. A situation has been created whereby the children are able to exercise and develop these hypothesis forming and supported argument skills. This is more than just facilitating, it is actually enhancing the learning situation and helping to take the thinking involved on to higher levels.

However, the Exploration group was just one of several in this class of children, just as the explorers themselves were part of a much wider society. The strengths and weaknesses in this model of classroom organization are examined in more detail in the final chapter, on 'Classroom Considerations'. One of the aspects considered there arises here: the bringing together of the in-depth investigations of the different groups to attempt to create that synthesis of their findings that is necessary for any real understanding of the period under study. The failure to achieve this will leave the children with both a distorted and an incomplete picture of the period they have been looking at. This 'breadth and depth' equation is one that continues to tax

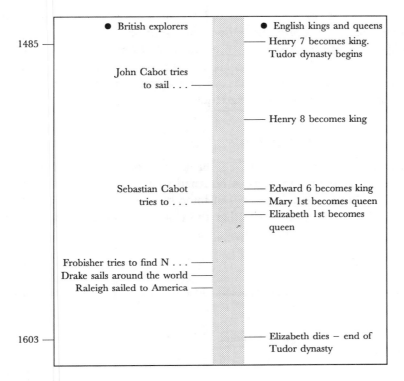

Figure 4.4

those involved in curriculum design and especially so in the wake of the National Curriculum. The early OFSTED reports rightly expressed concerns about the way the former had overshadowed the latter in the first years of the National Curriculum and their submissions (OFSTED, 1993a) to the Dearing Review (NCC/SEAC, 1993a) emphasized this and will have contributed to the slimmed Mark II version that followed.

Synthesis, the bringing together of the component parts, is a challenge for all historians whatever their level of study, but is vital in the primary classroom. I suggest that IT, and particularly the computer-based timeline, has a further contribution to make here. If one assumes that each of the groups has been working on their own area of study in a similar way to the Exploration group they too will have entered their key findings on to their own timeline disk. What the best of the computer timelines programs enable you to do is to merge these individual files, thus establishing a master disk with all the information from the different sub-groups under appropriate headings: monarchs, religion, country life, town life, leisure, transport, houses were some that were suggested earlier that might co-exist with the explorers.

As can be seen in Figures 4.3 and 4.4, it is possible for any two of the different data files (using the individual group headings) to be presented alongside each other on the screen at the same time and in relation to each other. This *relating* of one thing to another is a very significant step forward in supporting the development of this synthesis which is necessary for any deeper understanding of the events being studied.

Developing an IT capability

The contribution the use of IT in the above context might make to each child's developing IT capability is returned to and explored in greater depth in the final chapter. However, it is of interest to note just some of the aspects of the IT Programme of Study that the example considered in this chapter might reasonably claim to be making a contribution to.

Pupils should have opportunities to:

1a

use IT to explore and solve problems in the context of work across a variety of subjects;

1b

use IT to further their understanding of information that they have retrieved and processed;

2c

examine and discuss their experiences of IT, and assess its value in their working practices;

2d

investigate parallels with the use of IT in the wider world, consider the effects of such uses, and compare them with other methods.

Pupils should be taught to:

2a

use IT equipment and software to communicate ideas and information in a variety of forms, incorporating text, graphs, pictures and sound, as appropriate, showing sensitivity to the needs of their audience;

2b

use IT equipment and software to organise, reorganise and analyse ideas and information;

2c

select suitable information and media, and classify and prepare information for processing with IT, checking for accuracy;

2d

interpret, analyse and check the plausibility of information held on IT systems, and select the elements required for particular purposes, considering the consequences of any errors.

(IT, PoS, KS2; DFE, 1995)

The contention throughout these pages has been that the IT and history interaction is a two-way one with benefits accruing to both. The opportunities created by using IT in the context of history studies touches all of the above in varying degrees. It is also worth noting here that the above list is some two-thirds of the IT programme of study for this Key Stage. However, it is important not to claim too much for any one curriculum area when considering how and where the development of the children's IT capability might occur. At the same time it is just as important to ensure that all the *possible* opportunities are identified – and history offers many.

Conclusion

So what exactly is the contribution of IT to both the creation of and the dynamics of the situations created above, with children collecting, collating and then further reflecting upon the information they have to advance their understanding? To understand this one really needs to pause for a moment and leave the classroom behind and think about the use of IT in the wider world including business and economics. Why is IT used so extensively here? What is its contribution? Although there are specific uses there is one that stands out, and that is what is often referred to as 'number crunching'! This is a colloquial term for the computer's ability to handle massive amounts of data and to manipulate it at fantastic speeds, now so fast that new units of time have had to be invented to describe them. This data might be addresses, ages, bank accounts, CD sales, computer ownership, or almost anything! However, it is not the ability to store the data that is so important now but the ability to relate the different elements of the stored information to each other, singly or in multiples. This ability to ask 'Is there a relationship between . . .?' is a very important one in many walks of life. The ability to ask the question is not new – the ability to have the answer provided within seconds is unprecedented. I say that the ability to ask the question or pose the hypothesis is not new and this is obviously true as it is is a human characteristic, but it is not quite that simple. The speed with which one's questions/hypotheses can be addressed by the computer and a response obtained is likely to lead to more questions being asked, and I suggest of a more complicated and involved nature. The computer therefore is not acting merely as a tool to support existing thinking but is also acting as a *catalyst* to develop this thinking in ways that would not have occurred if it had been absent. That is, its presence doesn't just support thinking but actually contributes to its development. This was what Papert (1980) was talking about when he referred to the computer contributing to the qualitative dimension of the users' thinking (as discussed in the opening chapter).

Is this replicated in the learning situation, and particularly in the primary school? I would wish to argue in the affirmative. The control the children in the Exploration group have over their data once they have put it into the computer reflects the examples from the world of commerce above. It is the control over the variables that empowers them as they discuss their observations and ideas, seeking to draw a conclusion or two if it can be supported by the evidence available. Discussions involving phrases like 'Let's see if . . .', 'I wonder if . . .', 'Did everyone want the same things then?' are more likely to be asked if the information needed to provide the answers is readily and *easily* available. I have never subscribed to the 'If it's going to do you good it's got to hurt' argument that is often rehearsed at this stage, whether the issue be calculators in maths or spellcheckers in language work. If one has sound educational aims that one is seeking to achieve, anything that makes these more readily achievable for increasing numbers of children has my support. My own early experiences in using the computer with primary aged children and my realization of its potential contribution as a catalyst in the development of these higher-level thinking skills is documented elsewhere (Smart, 1988).

Earlier in the chapter the Key Elements of the National Curriculum for history were reviewed. It was seen how these are intended to develop the children's knowledge of, skills in and understanding of the process of historical enquiry as they work on the content of the study units of which the Tudor Life of this chapter is one example. The elements are quite explicit on the vital importance of the need to be able to impose some sort of order on the mass of information that is available for any one period of history. They state that:

Pupils should be taught:

to place the events, people and changes in the periods studied within a chronological framework.

to recall, select and organise historical information.

to describe and make links between the main events, situations and changes both within and across periods.

to describe and identify reasons for and results of historical events, situations, and changes in the periods studied.

how to find out about aspects of the periods studied, from a range of resources of information.

to ask and answer questions, and to select and record information relevant to a topic.

to communicate their knowledge and understanding of history in a variety of ways. (Key Elements, KS2; DFE, 1995)

These are quite explicit in their requirements about helping child i develop the skills necessary for organization. The rationale for this is simp.y an acknowledgement that it is a necessary prerequisite for them to move more confidently into the area of asking/posing those questions/hypotheses that take them on to an *understanding of* rather than just a *knowledge of.*

At the outset of this chapter the historical concept of chronology was explored. It was seen how the development of chronological frameworks, both within and across historical periods, is considered necessary to move towards developing that ultimate aim of historical understanding. The children involved in the Exploration group would have been using and developing their historical skills as they identified the information they required, decided where to seek it, determined whether it could be considered reliable, etc. In the process their own individual and collective knowledge base would be slowly widening. The claim made above for the contribution of IT in this small example is that it provided a means of the children having greater organizational and interrogative power over the information on the explorers of the Tudor period than is available by other means. As such it facilitated what was being aimed for anyway in the creating of a chronological framework for the voyages of exploration that took place. However, as this process was taking place the organizational support provided by the use of IT created a situation whereby it was possible for the children to more readily see the relationship between the individual voyages and wider exploratory movement that each was part of. This, of itself, created a situation whereby questions and hypotheses were more likely to be asked and posed. In this way it not only facilitated but enhanced the learning process underway and helped take the children's knowledge, skills and understanding of history and of this particular period of history further than would have been the case without the use of IT.

The children and their teachers of the 1990s have the tremendous advantage over earlier generations in not only having a sound and clear model of history in school to work to but, in IT, a new and powerful range of tools which increases their chances of success in realizing these aims.

References

Bartholomew, A. and Ramsey, T. (1990) *Time Lines*. Warminster: Soft-Teach.

Bruner, J. (1963) *The Process of Education*. New York: Vintage Books.

Bruner, J. (1966) *Towards a Theory of Instruction*. New York: Harvard University Press.

Bruner, J. (1983) *Child's Talk*. London: Oxford University Press.

Bruner, J. (1986) *Actual Minds, Possible Worlds*. London: Harvard University Press.

Byth, J. (1990) *History 5–9*. London: Hodder & Stoughton.

Cooper, H. (1992) *The Teaching of History*. London: Fulton.

DES (1985) *History in the Primary and Secondary Years: An HMI View.* London: HMSO.

DES (1986) *History from 5–16: Curriculum Matters 11. An HMI Series.* London: HMSO.

DES (1989a) *Aspects of Primary Practice: The Teaching and Learning of History.* London: HMSO.

DES (1989b) *National Curriculum: History Working Group Interim Report.* London: DES.

DES (1990) *National Curriculum: History Working Group Final Report.* London: DES.

DES (1991a) *History in the National Curriculum.* London: HMSO.

DES (1991b) *History Non-statutory Guidance.* London: HMSO.

DFE (1995) *Key Stages 1 and 2 of the National Curriculum.* London: DFE.

Donaldson, M. (1978) *Children's Minds.* London: Fontana.

ESM (1991) *Time Traveller.* Cambridge: Living and Learning.

Hallam, R. (1967) Logical thinking in history. *Educational Review* **19**(2), 183–202.

Jahoda, G. (1963) Children's concept of time and history. *Educational Review* **15**(2), 87–104.

Lello, J. (1980) The concept of time, the teaching of history and school organisation. *History Teacher* **13**(3).

NCC/SEAC (1993a) *The National Curriculum and Its Assessment: An Interim Report by Sir Ron Dearing.* London: HMSO.

NCC/SEAC (1993b) *The National Curriculum and Its Assessment: Final Report.* London: HMSO.

OFSTED (1993a) *Curriculum Organisation and Classroom Practice in Primary Schools: A Follow up Report.* London: OFSTED.

OFSTED (1993b) *The National Curriculum: Possible Ways Forward.* London: OFSTED.

Papert, S. (1980) *Mindstorms: Children, Computers and Powerful Ideas.* Hemel Hempstead, Herts: Harvester Press.

Peel, E. (1967) 'Some problems in the psychology of history teaching', in W.H. Burston and D. Thompson (eds), *Studies in the Nature and Teaching of History.* London: Routledge & Kegan Paul.

Smart, L. (1988) The database as a catalyst. *Journal of Computer Assisted Learning* **4**(3), 140–149.

Smith, L. and Tomlinson, P. (1977) The development of children's construction of historical duration. *Educational Research* **19**(3), 163–170.

Vygotsky, L.S. (1962) *Thought and Language.* New York: Wiley.

Wells, G. (1987) *The Meaning Makers.* London: Hodder & Stoughton.

West, J. (1978) Young children's awareness of the past. *Trends in Education* **1**, 8–15.

West, J. (1981) Primary school children's perception of authenticity and time in historical narrative pictures. *Teaching History* **29**, 8–10.

Wood, D., Bruner, J. and Ross, G. (1976) The role of tutoring in problem solving. *Journal of Child Psychology* **17**(2), 89–100.

CHAPTER 5
Classroom Considerations

History and IT are important parts of the primary curriculum, but they are only parts contributing to the whole. Both of these points are self-evident once made, but it is important to acknowledge them at the beginning of this final chapter. Neither IT nor history exists in a vacuum and although they have been considered in their own right within the covers of this book, it has been noted throughout that they form part of a much wider picture. Any of the ideas or suggestions arising from the examples of the previous chapters need to be taken by the individual teacher and applied to his/her own classroom and children. This 'taking of ownership' of any idea is necessary for it to be used in any situation other than the one it was originally presented in. As individual teachers come across new ideas from discussions with colleagues, INSET or other courses, from their own further studies and books they read, they have to consider how the new will fit into the existing situation. If it seems as if the innovation will not only fit but will also contribute to the more effective achievement of those wider educational aims, there is every chance of it being incorporated. This successful innovation agenda was explored in Chapter 1.

In this final chapter it is the intention to explore some of the wider, and practical, issues that a teacher with a primary class will have to address as he or she seeks to use IT successfully in the teaching of history. These would include the implications for classroom management, issues like differentiation and access, equal opportunities, matters such as progression and continuity, links with other curriculum areas, assessment and record keeping. However, the intention is not merely to show how these can be addressed or overcome so that progress can be made in the use of IT in history. Rather it is also an attempt to show, or at least suggest, how the use of IT in history projects can actually make a contribution to progress in these wider areas as well. This acknowledges the dynamic nature of classroom life, whereby change in one area often leads to change in another – or at least a re-evaluation of the existing state of affairs.

A detailed treatment of any of the above requires a book in its own right and these can be readily found but, in a decade when the primary curriculum (here used in its widest and encompassing sense) has had to endure tremendous fragmentary pressures, it is important to draw attention to the interwoven nature and to keep sight of the whole.

Classroom management, IT and history

In this section the intention is to focus on some of the classroom management issues that will arise and need to be addressed when IT is used in history-based topics such as those considered in the previous chapters.

With a class of 30 or more children how does a teacher create situations whereby the children can become familiar with the relevant computer programs, have equal access to them, have the time to actually explore what contribution the computer can make to their investigations/presentations and, importantly, enable them to reflect upon its contribution to their studies? The importance of this last point was discussed in Chapter 1 when the concept of developing an IT capability as opposed to merely using a computer was explored. Although there are a considerable number of schools who bring all their computers together in a computer lab, the norm is now to find at least one and often two computers in each primary classroom. The combination of computer labs and one/two computers in each classroom is likely to become more common as the numbers of machines in schools slowly creeps up, and there are definite advantages to a combined model. Here, however, the focus is on the classroom. I would contend that one/two computers are quite adequate for any of the examples considered in the previous pages and that primary teachers may not be too keen to have more than two or three even if finance allows such to be considered in the future. The British primary classroom is quite distinctive and is the result of a long period of evolutionary development. The evolutionary nature of this is, I suggest, of great significance at the present time and has meant that the quite unprecedented pressures from politicians and their appointees to move to a more subject-based and teacher-directed model in the 1990s did not have the impact expected by them (OFSTED, 1994). Nevertheless these pressures continue to be exerted (OFSTED, 1995). The assertiveness of those advocating the changes in practice has not, to date, been substantiated by sufficient quality evidence in relation to the effectiveness of any one particular method. Indeed, the 'Three Wise Men' (DES, 1992a) who had been specifically charged with 'concluding the debate about effective teaching methods in the primary school' by the then Secretary of State for Education, Kenneth Clarke, singularly failed to do so. Their recommendation that teachers and schools should systematically review their practice to ensure organization and teaching strategies were contributing to the effective realization of their aims was, however, both appropriate and timely.

By the the mid-1990s it was reluctantly acknowledged that it was simply not possible to create a viable and workable curriculum model with accompanying assessment arrangements without involving teachers in the design of these. The second version of the National Curriculum was based on a massive consultation exercise with the profession (NCC/SEAC, 1993a), with teachers then playing the leading part in all the subsequent working groups set up to advise on the modifications. When reflecting upon the almost total exclusion of the same in the drawing up of the first version, it is not surprising that it was found to be so seriously flawed. As has been seen, 1995 saw the introduction of the Mark II version of the National Curriculum and a promise that it would remain stable at least until the year 2000. This stability will hopefully help create a situation whereby a *more considered and reflective analysis* of what we know about the factors which contribute to maximizing the effectiveness of the teaching and learning can be undertaken.

If, as seems likely (OFSTED, 1995), the next aspect of education to come under the spotlight is teaching methods, it is to be hoped that the necessary lesson will have been learned from the above and teachers will be involved from the outset.

The quote from the Hadow Report on Primary Education (1931) is now over 60 years old but the message remains as relevant today as when it was first written:

> The primary school has its own canons of excellence and criteria of success: it must have the courage to stand by them. (Hadow; Board of Education, 1931)

All the examples used in the earlier chapters were or could be undertaken within an ordinary primary classroom and any of the difficulties and potential problems have to be tackled within this context. Although there is certainly not one model, British primary classrooms do generally share certain features (Alexander, 1992) which are indicative of an approach to teaching and learning. I don't think it is inappropriate to say that a primary classroom is akin to a multi-faceted workshop with a wide range of fundamental equipment to support the different activities the children will be engaged in over the day or the week. Common features are likely to include some, but probably not all, of the following:

- the reading area – comfortable and quiet, with a reference section and collection of literature, possibly with a tape recorder and headphones to enable stories to be listened to;
- the art area – usually close to the sink with a range of media, paint, material, junk and equipment including brushes, glues, art shirts or aprons, all usually located away from the main book areas;
- the children's drawer units or similar with the communal collection of rulers, colouring pencils and felt tip pens, different paper for drafting, sketching or geometric work, usually in an accessible location;
- the interest table with a focus on the current topic and/or with items the children have brought in because they thought they would be of interest;

- the displays around the room – usually representing the children's work in different curriculum areas currently being studied.

The intention is to create an impression here rather than a detailed inventory, but other features might well include writing corners equipped with a range of papers and pens; workbays for different subject areas; ongoing experiments on window sills; cages and tanks of gerbils, guinea pigs and fish, etc. None of the above, or combination of the above, would be considered unusual.

As was stated above it is not suggested that all of these features co-exist at any one time in every classroom, but they are all features that would easily be found on a visit to most primary schools anywhere in the country. The computer has had to fit into this existing framework and I would suggest this has increasingly been a successful integration. The point being established is that any more than two computers in a classroom would simply not be appropriate without disturbing this fine equilibrium that most primary teachers skilfully manage to maintain. In the following pages it will be suggested that this integration of the computer into the primary classroom and primary classroom life is the basis of its present success and future development. There is scope to ask if there are any lessons to be learned from this and why the increasingly rich and varied IT experience that many children are now experiencing in their primary schooling is frequently failing to be developed when they move on to secondary education, where a very different philosophy and model usually prevails. This, however, is beyond the scope of this present book.

This form of organization of the (hypothetical) primary classroom outlined above reflects the working practices of those operating within it. It implies, for example, that there will be times when not all the children will engage in the same activity at the same time. One needs to add 'usually' here, as flexible arrangements for borrowing equipment from neighbouring classrooms to support more children in any one activity invariably exist. The range of activities undertaken at any one time varies not only between classrooms but also within any single one. The phrase used in the so-called 'Three Wise Men' report by Alexander, Rose and Woodhead (DES, 1992a) of *fitness for purpose*, with teachers devising and varying their organizational strategies to support their intended learning outcomes, remains a useful one.

This organizational approach with different groups of children working on different curriculum areas or different aspects of the same curriculum area has, I believe, definite advantages for maximizing the use that can be made of the computer in the classroom.

One of the initial difficulties that faces any teacher, of whatever degree of IT experience or confidence, is the introduction of a new program to a class of children. The examples in the previous chapters, whether it be a database or integrated word-processing package or a CD-ROM or a timeline program, all pose this difficulty. Different teachers will have their own strategies for tackling this and as long as it is successful that's fine. However, I would like to mention one method that was or could be used in any of the previous chapters and which addresses the two most problematic areas. The first of these is the *number of children* in a class who need to be introduced to a program and taken to a stage where they can begin to use it with a basic degree of confidence and competence. The second factor is the limited amount of *teacher time* that is available when all the other demands upon it are considered.

Elsewhere (Smart, 1992) I referred to the following method as *the snowball approach* and as this captures the essence and spirit of the approach I shall continue to use it here. If the reader is interested in a more detailed consideration she is referred to the above reference. It developed as a practical response to the two key factors above; a large class and not enough time. It is basically a very simple and certainly not original model that operates as follows:

Having familiarized him/herself with the rudiments of the new program prior to introducing it to the class the teacher initially works with three children at the computer showing them its key features. This would include how to enter data in the examples on Victorians and Tudors, how to move around the program, whether by mouse click or text entry, how to save and print work − generally to play with the program. This 'playing with' might sound strange to some ears, but that is what we all do with a new piece of equipment, computer program or otherwise (hi-fi unit, TV, mobile phone, etc.). It is a key part of the familiarization process through which there are no short cuts when seeking long-term effective use of a program.

The next stage is to introduce a sense of purpose. In the Victorians/local study project the use of a census on a database program was explored and is used as the example of the snowball approach here. Assuming the children have looked at the original enumerator's sheets, discussed the information there and that the headings for entering the data under have been agreed (again see Smart, 1992 for alternatives), the time comes when the children are ready to enter their own data as taken from the enumerator's returns. The first group of children work closely with the teacher and enter their own data. As the first child enters her data the group is encouraged to discuss and attempt to sort out any problems they encounter, but the teacher is close at hand. As the data begin to be entered (perhaps three entries from the originals each) the teacher takes a step back but remains easily available to provide key bits of support as and when necessary to help achieve the desired *basic* competence and resulting confidence for the children in this first group. Once the first child has entered her data she leaves and a new child joins in

107

the *novice role*, but working alongside two *experts*. This new child would be briefed by the other two and then observe one enter her data. This one would then leave and another child join, meaning the novice had now progressed to being the second most experienced person in the trio. And so this approach moves through the whole class and all the children come to use and develop this basic competence and basic confidence with the new program. Data entry is perhaps the least educationally valuable aspect of using the database, but without it there is no chance of creating a situation whereby the teacher can start to explore its potential contribution to the development of the children's knowledge and skills in history.

Although the Victorian database is used as the example here, it could as easily have been the timeline from the Tudor topic or the CD-ROM from the Vikings – or indeed any program not used in these examples. The issue here is the classroom management one and it can be seen how such a method offers two advantages. Firstly, the teacher is not tied to the computer group but becomes increasingly free to devote his attention elsewhere; secondly, the act of observing and then having to explain the procedures to a peer certainly seems to enhance the understanding developed by each child. When a problem or difficulty did occur, as it inevitably did, it also meant that there was an increasing number of *experts* who could be called upon to help rather than just the teacher. Indeed, in my own experience, some children became increasingly more knowledgeable than myself in relation to specific programs and I would often call upon them to help sort out a difficulty or explore an alternative; and I found that increasingly they didn't necessarily wait to be called upon but would offer their ideas unsolicited. This is an example of the dynamic which the use of IT introduces into the classroom with its potential to modify and offer challenges to existing working relationships. The *reaction* to it will vary depending upon the teacher's approach to learning and how the teacher/learner relationship is perceived, but the latent features remain.

A second key aspect of the classroom management agenda when using computers in the way envisaged in the previous chapters is access to the computer for each child within the class. As was seen in Chapter 1, all children are required to develop an IT capability as defined by the National Curriculum. In the same chapter it was also seen how this capability was expected to be developed across the whole range of curriculum areas. Schools will increasingly be required to audit each child's IT experience and to map or plan which strand of this IT capability is being developed where. History has a major contribution to make to this for, although the main emphasis in this book has been on how IT contributes to the development of the child's historical knowledge, skills and understanding, so every attempt has also been made to illustrate how this, *at the same time*, contributes to developing the IT capability. The latter cannot be developed without a context and history offers many.

At the classroom level each child's IT experience needs to be planned for rather than left to chance, otherwise some children are likely to be disadvantaged in the development of their IT capability. With the one/two computers in the classroom scenario outlined above, it is suggested that all the examples used in this book create situations whereby all the children in a given class will need to use the computer in their different investigations or to communicate their findings. In some situations, as in the data entry one discussed above, a systematic approach can be created whereby everyone is involved in a basic task and with it a basic skill. However, what must always be remembered here is that this is no more than a means to an end. As was explored in detail in the previous chapters, it is what IT *adds* to the teaching of history in the primary school that makes its use so exciting. Examples were seen where the manipulation of large amounts of data that would be beyond them in any any other form gave children the power to ask more, and more involved questions of the data and to pose hypotheses in relation to their enquiries. Further examples sought to illustrate how the particularly difficult problem of providing opportunities for children to work with primary source material when studying the more distant past might be overcome to some extent by the use of CD-ROM. Again this was seen as only a first step, as the power it then gave to ask questions of this information was where IT really began to contribute to the development of their knowledge, skills and understanding.

Access to the computer is likely to remain a problem if it is perceived as requiring all the children in the class to have exactly equal amounts of time or as requiring them to have identical experiences (that is, to use the same program in the same way for the same purposes). In the early days of computer use in the classroom this was what was often aimed for, leading to rotas for going on the computer with usually strict time allocations. I can remember supervising a student on teaching practice where her teacher used a rota such as the one above. Groups of children were allocated a time, 20 minutes at the computer, where they were working with a program called Granny's Garden. One group were having an involved discussion about a decision that had to be made in relation to the problem posed by one of the characters. From across the room the teacher suggested that they 'stopped talking all the time and got on with it because it would be time for the next group in five minutes!' So they did, but as the discussion ceased, so did the quality of the learning.

As was seen in the opening chapter, the IT capability that the National Curriculum requires each child to develop during Key Stage 2 begins with the statement

Pupils should be taught to extend the range of IT tools that they use for communication, investigation and control; *become discerning in their use of IT*; *select* information, sources, and media for their *suitability for purpose*; and *assess the value* of IT in their working practices. (IT, PoS; DFE, 1995b)

The emphases are mine, but it is quite clear that central to this notion of an IT capability is that the individual child will exercise a degree of control over when he/she makes use of the computer to support his/her present task. This must be an informed decision and for it to be so obviously requires an awareness of, and basic knowledge of how to use any particular program. As programmers continue to make it ever easier to use the programs [i.e. the Microsoft CD-ROM *Ancient Lands* (1994) requires a mere four mouse clicks on easily identifiable icons to be able to get to use the program and all its features], the time and effort required to take children to this basic level of competency will almost disappear. The snowball approach outlined above may continue to make a contribution, but it is likely that the competence/confidence development equation may be reversed, with the latter becoming the main reason for its continued use.

The implications for children's access to the class computer(s) as considered here will therefore lead increasingly to a situation whereby the onus will be on the child or the group of children to determine whether they will use the computer rather than being directed to it by the teacher. The teacher's role in relation to computer usage in his/her classroom will be to create and present tasks whereby the children have to make decisions about whether the computer can make a contribution to their successfully completing the task in the best possible way. Indeed, hearing a group of children decide that 'the computer's going to be no use for this . . .' could be clear evidence that the desired IT capability is at an advanced stage of development! This situation, far from diminishing the teacher's role, actually makes it more important than ever. It means that that central skill of being able to create challenging, meaningful and purposeful learning situations and then to provide appropriate measures of support to enable each child to achieve and communicate success, is being employed.

In the chapter on Tudor Life it was seen how the way of storing relevant data in an organized and accessible way in the initial stages later became a resource in its own right that the children could refer to if and when they thought appropriate. There were parallel examples in the use of the census material in the Victorian period/local study topic where decisions had to be made by the children as to whether to see if the computer or some other resource might be most useful at that stage of their enquiry. There will certainly be times in most classrooms when more than one child or group of children want to use the computer at the same time. There will be other times when the computer hums quietly away in the corner with no one seeking to use it. This is implicit in the above. Children will occasionally have to wait or do something else for the moment or see if the computer in the resource area or next-door classroom can be used. This is part and parcel of primary classroom life, but where one sees it happening it is a sign of how far the integration of the computer into this framework has been achieved.

One final point before leaving this section on access, and this concerns time. In the examples of the previous chapters it is almost impossible to say how much time each task or group of children working on the task would require at the computer. Sometimes it will be no more than a few minutes to check or confirm a simple fact date, name, relationship, etc., while at others it may involve pursuing a line of enquiry, finding it unproductive, retracing one's steps and setting off in another direction. The making of decisions, to become discerning, to evaluate alternatives before selecting, to decide upon suitability for purpose, to be able to assess the value as determined by the IT capability of the National Curriculum all require time. I would suggest that the time allocation of the rota type referred to above was never really appropriate for supporting effective learning and will have no real part to play in the development of the desired IT capability.

One can see how this is another example of IT having an impact on the wider learning environment and its organization. The onus moves from the teacher directing the child or group of children to use the computer to the latter determining whether it, or some other tool, will best serve their present purposes. But, as was noted earlier, it is not as simply 'linear' as this. The power over the information itself opens up the opportunities for seeing what can be done with it – it actively encourages the posing of 'I wonder if . . .' type questions; and of course, because the questions themselves could not be anticipated in advance, the answers are difficult to have prepared. The teacher as sole source of knowledge has never been a sustainable or even an honest one and the use of IT will make it even less so. If the realization of the IT capability envisaged by the National Curriculum (DFE, 1995b) is to be achieved, teachers will increasingly have to be prepared to come to terms with this. All teachers have at some time become involved with an experiment in science or an examination of an old map or an attempt to mix a certain colour tone where they become a learner themselves, trying things out, unsure of the results, tolerating failure and maybe celebrating success. Not only are such experiences satisfying, but they are often exciting because working together the teacher and child interact as learners pushing at frontiers of knowledge, skills or understanding. I suggest that the increasing use of IT will create more and more situations of this type. The examples of the previous chapters have concentrated on this taking place in the curriculum area of history but of course the above developments are having and will continue to have a much wider influence. It is another example of the dynamic that IT brings to the learning situation and its power to not only contribute to it but to affect it as well.

Differentiation and access

Although now very much part of the educational lexicon in the 1990s, differentiation is a relatively new arrival (Weston, 1992). The DES discussion document *Better Schools* of 1985 seems to be where it first made its public debut, appearing alongside 'breadth', 'balance' and 'relevance' as fundamental principles to inform curriculum planning. The Educational Reform Act (1988) with its entitlement model of the curriculum placed differentiation right at the heart of the National Curriculum, making it quite explicit that this was not only a desirable feature but a required one.

> Within any group of pupils there will be a wide range of ability and experience. This calls for a flexible approach allowing for differentiation to provide success and challenges for them all. (NCC, 1989)

This is now reflected in the inspection criteria for schools where evidence of differentiation is expected (OFSTED, 1994). Differentiation is often linked with children with learning difficulties but this is to misunderstand and underestimate its relevance. Much more useful and productive, I suggest, is to link it with the earlier concept of *match* (i.e. Harlen, 1982) or with Vygotsky's (1978) *zone of proximal development* (ZPD), with teachers attempting to set or develop tasks that challenge and stretch children, moving them on from their existing levels of knowledge, skills and understanding. This of course links directly with the points made above about the role of the teacher in attempting to maximize the effectiveness of each child's learning (Bennett *et al.*, 1984). Differentiation of course can only take place in a context and it is suggested that the use of IT in the teaching and learning of history actually creates many opportunities for the creation of differentiated learning experiences. Although much more involved in practice, differentiation is usually conceived of as taking place through the task set, the resources used or the outcomes expected. These are not exclusive of each other and attention to one aspect often has implications for another (i.e. differentiation by task can often have implications for the resources used).

None of the areas considered in this chapter can be dealt with in depth and the reader is referred elsewhere for this (i.e. Weston, 1992), but it is possible to identify where opportunities for differentiation were present in the examples considered in the previous chapters. The awareness of how such opportunities can be planned for or can be activated when they arise, rather than any attempt to replicate the ones used, is the reason for including them here. For illustration, one example is taken from each of the three topic chapters.

Consider for a moment the Victorian England/local study. The basic organization of the children was in groups working on different aspects of life during this period in their locality. The use of the Key Question approach and the focus on the paired concepts of similarity and difference, continuity and change and cause and effect had formed the framework for each group's investigations.

The group investigating 'Jobs Now and Jobs Then' was a mixed-ability one in terms of the children's ability to take information from and communicate their thoughts and ideas through the written form: in lay terms, there were some children who had quite serious difficulties with their reading and writing. As is often the case, however, the same children's ability to communicate verbally far outstripped their limitations with the written word. This was a very keen and enthusiastic group and they had had some very lively discussion about what they were looking for as they looked at jobs and they discussed how they might use the database with the census material on to find out more. Initially they printed out the whole file with names, ages, sex and occupations. They had more information than they now needed and the irrelevant parts were getting in the way. The suggestion to just print out the jobs came from one of the less able readers and writers and was well received, and she was asked if she could go and do that by others in the group. She asked the other member of the group with similar reading and writing difficulties to go with her to help. Noticing this pairing at the keyboard I went over with a general 'what are you after?' and was told they were going to try to print out 'just the jobs'. A brief discussion took place about what they were going to do with the information and it became clear that the whole group was engaged in trying to establish which were the most common jobs in 1871 and this had been further refined to 'for men and for women'. With almost no further help they went through several printouts, gradually narrowing the headings under which the lists appeared to 'sex' and 'occupations'. Pronunciation of some of the jobs was problematic but this was not central to this enquiry with its focus on the number and frequency. I enquired what they intended to do next and they said they intended to go through the list counting up how many there were of each type and then see whether they were done by men or women. It was obvious from their voice tone that this sounded a little daunting.

'Can the computer be of any more help?' I enquired, or rather prompted.

'Could we have all the same jobs together so that we can count them more easily?' was the reply.

'Better still, can we have all the men's and women's jobs together?' added her partner.

In discussion, and with a little help with the necessary SORT command, this was achieved and the two returned to their group triumphant. Several 'wows' and 'how do you do that?' and 'that's saved us hours!' confirmed the contribution they had made. Also of great importance to these two children was that they had had their contribution acknowledged.

The collection of this sorted data was of course only a stage in the investigation into the 'what was different?' and into the more difficult question of 'why was it different ?' that the group moved on to. The use of the IT had enabled the children to process the necessary data quickly and easily and had freed them to move to the higher-level questions. The opportunity it provided for children with learning difficulties to play a full and significant part in this process was dramatic. The presence of IT enabled them to have access to the relevant information in a way that meant their difficulties with the written word did not prevent them using and handling the questions and concepts that were quite within their grasp. The impact it had on their own self-concepts is another matter but it is worthy of note that they became informal consultants to other groups in the class who wanted to have their data presented in a range of formats.

This is just one very small-scale example among many that could have been chosen. I use this particular one because of the insight it gave me as the teacher into how the presence of IT seemed to make it easier to *fine tune* the tasks presented or agreed with the children. The level of sophistication could easily be adjusted in terms of the initial question posed or the direction the investigation proceeded along or of what evidence might be sought. That is, the task, the outcome or the resources (here referring to the data that was worked on) could be modified at either the planning stage prior to the lessons or could easily be modified within the lesson itself in response to the teacher's evaluation of individuals' and groups' progress. What is also demonstrated by the above example is how the computer enabled the teacher to also adjust the size of the steps that each child was required to make as their skills and understanding developed. An awareness of the importance of small achievable steps is central for teachers working with any children, but is even more important when working with children with learning difficulties. What was so exciting here was that the work on the central concepts, the questions and the chance to pose hypotheses were now more accessible to all the children. The flexibility and adaptability of the resource was a key factor in this contribution. Similar examples from the Tudor timeline program and perhaps even more easily from the CD-ROM use in the Vikings topic could also be identified. Although space prevents a detailed examination of these here, the reader is invited to speculate as to how the ease with which events and personalities from different aspects of Tudor life can be juxtaposed and related to each other could lead to questions and hypotheses being posed about the possible causes and effects between these. Or perhaps to consider how the ease with which a child could move from a reconstruction of a Viking house to a *series* of views of the archaeological dig is likely to enhance his/her understanding of the 'how do we know that' question, while also perhaps leading to one I heard asked, 'Yeah, OK but how do they know that the roof looked like that then?' And in the last example not a word needed to be written and the written text *supported* the information given rather than was the sole or even major way of accessing it.

I am not claiming that IT is the answer to differentiation and access in the primary classroom but I would argue that in the field of history it can certainly help teachers create and then explore opportunities that might be more difficult to do without it. Earlier in this chapter it was suggested that the issue of differentiation is most successfully tackled when it arises from the concept of 'match'. The tendency to link differentiation with Special Educational Needs (SEN) is, I suggest, to narrow its application to a section of each class of children, whereas match remains a more all-encompassing term. Appropriate use of IT can make an important contribution to this crucial aspect of creating successful learning situations (Smart, 1995).

Continuity and progression

A key part of the rationale for the introduction of the National Curriculum in the late 1980s was the contribution it would make to ensuring a greater degree of continuity and progression across schools, within schools and within the subject areas and topics undertaken there (DES, 1987b). Far easier to advocate and claim as opposed to actually demonstrate, it has nevertheless been seen as one of the early successes of the National Curriculum (OFSTED, 1994, 1995). Schools' and individual teachers' plans now attempt to build in continuity and progression in a much more explicit way and then to demonstrate their success through the achievements of the children.

The following definition was provided by the NCC to provide guidance here:

continuity . . . the planned provision of teaching, learning and other experiences which facilitate pupils' continuous development. (NCC, 1992)

The continuity that is so important to the creation of effective learning situations takes many forms. The physical environment and the people involved are just two aspects of this worthy of further consideration, but here the emphasis is on continuity in the curriculum. In the history curriculum the continuity is provided by the common approach to all the areas to be studied and is contained in the Key Elements section referred to in the previous chapters. The influence of Bruner (1966) and his spiral notion of the

115

curriculum, though rarely acknowledged, can be readily seen here. The use of a Key Question approach and certain central historical concepts (similarity and difference, continuity and change, cause and effect) as advocated in the previous chapters, further contributes to the achievement of greater continuity. This is not to suggest that this is the only possible approach, but rather to suggest that a common approach, however based, is an important part of creating continuity for those involved in the learning process, children and teachers alike.

Turning to IT, the continuity will probably manifest itself firstly through the actual computers the children work with within a school (the make and interface, mouse, keyboard style, etc., if not the exact machine specification). At the next level the continuity will probably occur through the software used within the school and its use with different age ranges. Some recent software (i.e. *First Word for Windows* by Research Machines, 1992) actually has different and increasingly more sophisticated operating levels built into it which can be brought into play at different stages and with different ages throughout the school years. The increased processing and storage power and particularly the greater use of CD-ROM certainly creates more opportunities for the inclusion of this facility and it will be interesting to see if it is taken. Whatever happens, the ability to feel comfortable with both the approach to the study being undertake and also with the actual machine and the program you are expected to work with, should not be underestimated.

PROGRESSION

> building systematically on pupils' knowledge, concepts, skills and attitudes to ensure development of their capabilities over a period of time. (NCC, 1992)

Progression is a more problematic concept and is probably most effectively developed when it arises from the foundations of continuity. HMI reports throughout the mid-1980s (HMI, 1989, 1990) make frequent reference to children underachieving because expectations of them were not high enough. In the HMI *Primary Schools: Some Aspects of Good Practice* (DES, 1987b) there is a section entitled 'Characteristics of Good Practice', in which HMI identify the teacher's concern to ensure progression in each child's learning as one of the most important factors in maximizing achievement. The National Curriculum assessment arrangements published in the following year were, and remain, an attempt to provide a structure for this to occur in a planned and systematic way. Originally these consisted of attainment targets made up of many statements of attainment which sought to identify in specific terms what children could do and to identify this against a level between 1 and 10 (DES, 1988). The Dearing Review (NCC/SEAC, 1993b) of the National Curriculum, which led to the reduction in content considered in earlier chapters, also led to the modification and simplification of the assessment arrangements. Much broader statements, known as 'level descriptions' of what a child can do are now used. Whether the simplification will lead to greater effectiveness in this field remains to be seen, but the revised system is certainly more manageable for teachers and this was perhaps the major consideration. Nevertheless, the rationale for the National Curriculum assessment model remains and this is to ensure that progression remains centre stage. The concepts of match and Vygotsky's zone of proximal development were considered briefly above and they have obviously informed these developments, although, again, it would be very difficult to find any acknowledgement of this in the official documents.

Progression is therefore part of both the history and the IT agenda. Children are expected to make progress in both the development of their knowledge, skills and understanding of history and in the development of their IT capability. Throughout the pages of this book the interaction of these two has been considered and how developments in one have a positive impact on the other and that this is a dynamic, ongoing process rather than a static, one-off, type. This is certainly the case in the area of progression. As with the other issues considered in this chapter a more in-depth treatment of the whole concept of progression must be sought elsewhere. However, the following example is presented to illustrate how IT can help teachers develop progression in their history teaching and of how, at the same time, history provides a context for the progressive development of an IT capability.

In the Tudor Life topic considered in Chapter 4, it was seen how the children used a computer timeline program. It was suggested that the use of this made a significant contribution to the development of the children's knowledge, skills and understanding in history in the following ways.

One of the keys to success in any historical enquiry is the ability to organize the available data in a way that keeps it accessible, both to use and to add to and to modify as the enquiry proceeds. For children this is particularly important if they are not to become swamped with the volume of information available. However, the 'to use' part has, I fear, often been overshadowed by the actual collection of the information itself, which has been allowed to become an end in itself. The Key Elements for Key Stage 2 provide clear guidance and expectations in relation to this. There is a section on Organization and communication which requires pupils

to recall, select and organise historical information, including dates and terms;

and in the Chronology section this organizational factor is more specific:

to place the events, people and changes in the periods studied within a chronological framework. (History, Key Elements, KS2; DFE, 1995b)

However, the *purpose* for this is quickly added and outlined. Under the sub-headings of 'range and depth of historical knowledge and understanding', 'interpretations of history' and 'historical enquiry', the following are required to be developed with pupils:

to describe and identify reasons for and results of historical events, situations, and changes in the periods studied.

to describe and and make links between the main events, situations and changes both within and across periods.

to identify and give reasons for different ways in which the past is represented and interpreted.

how to find out about aspects of the periods studied, from a range of resources of information . . .

to ask and answer questions, and to select and record information relevant to a topic. (Key Elements, KS2; DFE, 1995b)

It is suggested that the use of IT in history can make a significant contribution to promoting the desired progression in both areas of the curriculum in the following manner.

If one initially considers the collection and organization of information as outlined in the Elements (above). The Exploration group in Chapter 4 on Tudor Life were able to create a page (or several) of their own writing to accompany their timeline entry on Drake's circumnavigation of the world. There is no disputing that the text they entered in relation to their (key) questions could just as easily have been done on paper within a book or folder. However, this traditional form of recording information has two limitations. Firstly, either the best or final copy has to wait until all the required information is available in relation to, say, 'Why did Drake want to sail around the world?' or gaps have to be left, or it has to be rewritten at a future point. Using the power of the IT word processor (for this is what the text entry feature of the timeline package is) findings can be entered as they are found and even a comment on the state of the enquiry can be left in the text, in effect an *aide memoire*.

Below is a hypothetical but not unimaginable example from the group.

Drake left England in 1577. His ship was called the Golden Hind. He had four other ships with him. There were 166 sailors altogether.

NEXT *The question we all wanted to know but haven't been able to find out is did he mean to sail all the way around the world — we don't think he meant to sail round the world when he started off but we haven't found any evidence yet — Matthew is looking for it. He is going to see if Drake wrote any letters to the queen about this or if she gave him any orders.*

NEXT *thing to find out is how long he took (we think about 2 years) and which countries he went to.*

In relation to the development of the IT capability progression can be readily demonstrated with reference to the National Curriculum requirements for KS2.

Pupils should be given opportunities to:

use IT to organise, reorganise and analyse ideas and information.

select suitable information and media, and classify and prepare information for processing with IT, checking for accuracy.

use IT to further their understanding of information that they have retrieved and processed.

discuss their experiences of using IT and assess its value in their working practices. (IT, PoS, Key Stage 2; DFE, 1995b)

It is however in the widest sense that the use of IT in the above and similar examples is contributing to the the children's capability. A capability that must include not only being able to use IT but also to become discerning, selective, to determine suitability and to assess the value of IT in working practices (IT Programme of Study, DFE, 1995b). These longer-term aims, all part of the National Curriculum requirements, are the really important phrases for any true capability to be claimed. The small example above could form just one step among many towards this goal for as the guidance document *Approaches to IT Capability* (NCET, 1995), sent to each school, reminds teachers

IT capability builds slowly, over a period of time.

In relation to demonstrating progression in the development of their knowledge, skills and understanding the use of IT offers new opportunities to the teacher. One of the greatest difficulties in teachers' attempts to ensure progression is to actually identify where the child actually is in relation to the development of the desired skill or concept or knowledge which is the focus of attention. Often considerable attempts are made to establish where the children are at the outset of the studies being undertaken, but once underway most assessment takes place informally, often via conversations. This ongoing formative assessment is the bedrock of successful teaching but the sheer logistics of classroom life mean that the opportunities for those important interchanges between teacher and child or group of children are bound to be limited. I suggest that the opportunity provided by the use of the above computer program for the children to identify where they are and where they are going next is a wonderful one for both the children and the teacher. In terms of enhancing the learning situation by requiring some reflection upon where we have got to and prompting consideration of where we need to go next, it provides support in moving forward in the desired direction. It is also quite possible that this will lead to increased time on a task, and also to the further development of the children's collaborative learning skills by creating a purposeful context for them to be called upon.

This window into the group's development towards its agreed goals in relation to the *knowledge* about Drake, the *skills* of finding out how we know and the *understanding* of why he did what he did when he did it is provided by a reading of the screen or a printout. This is not impossible to achieve by other means but it has never been so easily accessible to the teacher.

As with any books or other work assessed by the teacher, the response to what the children hand in will be determined by many factors and will take a variety of forms, i.e. a written note, a verbal comment, etc. In this case it *could occasionally* take the form of a note left by the teacher on the NEXT section, making a suggestion . . ., i.e. 'A map of the route might be useful. (Miss Smith)'.

One final point here is also worthy of attention. Part of the development of children's IT capability is now seen as helping them to realize the parallels that exist between their use of IT in school and its use in the wider world (IT, PoS, DFE, 1995b). All of the above examples parallel how text is stored, often in an incomplete form, returned to later, modified before being read by someone else who contributes to it. However, for the children to come to realize this it will probably need to be discussed with them and the advantages and disadvantages of this, as opposed to other methods, considered. I can clearly remember the surprised looks on the faces of the children in my class when, during Book Week, a well-known author brought in his own drafting book and showed the children his notes, ideas and other scribbles that eventually led to the beautifully presented books we had in the reading corner. I'm sure that they thought drafting was something Sir had invented to make them work harder! Parallels with the wider world should, I suggest, be identified and discussed as and when the situations present themselves, for they are definitely a part of the developing IT capability. Along with other curriculum areas history makes a significant contribution by providing valuable and meaningful contexts.

ASSESSMENT

The whole issue of assessment and assessing progress is another that requires a treatment that is beyond the scope of this particular book. The rewrite of the National Curriculum that led to the Mark II version of 1995 was triggered ultimately by the unmanageable demands made by the previous model's assessment procedures. The revised version dramatically reduced the amount

120

and type of assessment that is now required with the role of ongoing, formative teacher assessment finally being acknowledged as being a central element (see Secretary of State's letter of introduction to the revised national curriculum, DFE, 1995a). The summative assessments now undertaken at the end of each Key Stage will continue to provide the broader overview.

However, one major element in the assessment process that has become increasingly important in recent years is the collection of evidence to support the assessments made and it is this aspect that is considered here. How does a teacher know what any child or group of children has come to know or understand or how well a new skill has developed? The increased emphasis and use of observation, profiles, learning records and conferencing since the late 1980s were an acknowledgement of the need to have more than just end products to base assessments on. Unfortunately all of these attempts to explore the process as well as the product make incredible demands upon that most valuable teacher commodity – time. What works in a small-scale pilot can become unmanageable when transferred to larger numbers of children and more curriculum areas, as was clearly demonstrated in the first SATs (Standard Assessment Tasks) undertaken by KS1 teachers in 1991.

Anything that contributes to gaining insights into children's developing knowledge, skills and understandings is likely to make a wider contribution to maximizing the effectiveness of the teaching and learning underway. The use of IT in the teaching of history can provide such insights *while at the same time* demonstrating the developing IT capability as outlined above and it needs to be remembered that the latter will always need a context.

The early years of the first model of the National Curriculum are likely to be remembered as the era of the 'tick chart' as teachers tried desperately to assess, monitor and then keep a record of each child's progress through the hundreds of statements of attainment. As has been seen, this impossible task was a key reason that led to the Dearing Review of 1994 and the revised orders of the following year. The quality of many assessments made under the previous system was questionable and one hopes that the requirement for less will contribute to enhancing the quality of the ones that take place from 1995 onwards.

The NCET (1995) guidance document captures this development and reminds teachers that

> It is no longer considered necessary to keep detailed records of assessments although teachers may find it beneficial to *record significant moves forward*.
> (NCET, 1995)

It then quotes with approval the pre-National Curriculum *Curriculum Matters 15 – Information Technology from 5–16* (DES, 1989) document:

> Everyday classroom activities provide the most effective setting for reliable evaluation of pupils' use of IT. (para. 94)

It is here suggested that the ability to print out a section or sections of any of the programs featured in the earlier chapters provides a further opportunity to acquire evidence of these significant moments/events to support the assessments made. As with evidence provided by children's drawings, writing and discussions held, it is the teacher's notes and annotations that identify the significance. Teachers have become increasingly knowledgeable in their understanding of the forms and purposes of different assessment techniques and increasingly skilful in their implementation in their classrooms and, as was noted above, this was acknowledged in the Secretary of State for Education's letter that accompanied the release of the new version.

As was identified in the examples considered in the previous chapters, there were many opportunities for teachers to collect evidence to support these assessments. Which opportunities are actually activated will require the exercise of the same skills teachers now use in relation to any other form of evidence and will obviously be related to the criteria being applied.

The interrelationship between IT and history can be clearly seen in the above. The combined picture and text advertisement of the Victorian house, the collection of pictures gathered on Viking household goods or the juxtaposition of explorers' journeys and new foods of the Tudor period on the timeline program could be selected as *significant* evidence of a child's progress in either history or in her IT capability. The *same* piece could of course be selected as evidence of progress in both areas at the same time!

In conclusion . . .

This last point brings us full cycle and returns us to the introductory chapter of this book where the claim was made that the use of IT in the teaching and learning of history in the primary classroom is a mutually beneficial one. The examples taken from children working on the Victorian/local study, the Tudors and the Vikings have sought to explore this claim in contexts which are both familiar and readily available to primary and middle school teachers across the country. The frequent references to the National Curriculum have been made for two purposes. Firstly, they acknowledge the operating situation for teachers in the second half of the 1990s and the framework within which they work with the children in their classes. Secondly, and just as important, has been the attempt to show that none of the National Curriculum developments in either IT or history or the relationship between them is solely dependent on the arrival of a National Curriculum in 1989.

Throughout, an attempt has been made to stress the evolutionary nature of primary education in this country and to identify developments in both IT and history prior to 1989. The influence these had on the working groups drawing up the new National Curriculum was very considerable. The National Curriculum then is perceived as another stage in the evolutionary development of primary education in England and Wales.

However, this is not to reduce its significance on developments in either the use of IT in history and the use of history to provide a context for the development of children's IT capability. I suggest that the National Curriculum has actually acted as a *catalyst* in this field and as such has had a very positive impact. The requirements that IT should feature in the teaching of primary school history and the requirements that IT should be perceived of as a cross-curricular skill have created a sound and very exciting base for present and future developments. Future developments that will see young children having access to materials and sources previously unimaginable and, perhaps more importantly, in new ways.

One might imagine a walk around Tutankhamen's burial suite with the ability to call up Carter's voice reading his own notes or to see photos taken of the original locations of the finds, to rotate them, to zoom in, to get a commentary from the leading expert of the day, etc. To then link up with a pupil in an Egyptian school for a video conference on the ideas and hypotheses being considered. Language difficulties? I don't think so – it will simply be a choice of touching the screen to identify input language and desired output language.

In fact, perhaps, as Papert (1980) suggested what seems a long time ago now, it is only the imagination that creates the limits as to what is possible. Crystal ball gazing is, however, a dangerous pastime and nowhere more so than in the field of technology with the rate of change as it is at present, and is one I make no claims for. In time this book will be superseded by others addressing the issues explored in these pages. They will almost certainly have sections on multimedia and the Internet and on developments that have yet to come to fruition.

And yet the central thrust of this book will still apply; namely that IT, in a variety of forms, can make a significant contribution to children's development in history. At the same time the child's awareness and understanding of the nature of IT is also advanced.

And, whether it is newspapers made on old BBC 'B' model computers or multimedia presentations on machines of almost undreamed of power and speed, the most significant factor in the use and release of this potential will continue to be the teacher. It is he or she who is, and will remain, the person who manages the whole learning environment and ensures a balance between all the facets of classroom life. The decisions he or she makes in relation to IT and history will be based on much wider educational considerations than merely those applying to these two areas.

In Chapter 1 it was suggested that a *second stage* of development in IT in schools had begun by the mid-1990s. If this is so the most significant feature of it is not the advances in the technology but rather in the *increased awareness* of an ever *increasing number* of teachers as to just what IT can contribute to the learning situations they seek to create in their classrooms.

The intention of this book has been to draw together, consolidate perhaps, and to offer some reflection on this interaction between IT and history in the context of the primary classroom as a contribution to this second stage.

References

Alexander, R. (1992) *Policy and Practice in Primary Education*. London: Routledge.

Bennett, N., Desforges, C. and Wilkinson, B. (1984) *The Quality of Pupil Learning Experiences*. London: Lawrence Erlbaum.

Board of Education (1931) *Report of the Consultative Committee on the Primary School (Hadow Report)*. London: HMSO.

Bruner, J.S. (1966) *Towards a Theory of Instruction*. New York: Norton.

DES (1987a) *Primary Schools: Some Aspects of Good Practice*. London: HMSO.

DES (1987b) *The National Curriculum 5–16: A Consultation Document*. London: HMSO.

DES (1988) *Task Group on Assessment and Testing: A Digest for Schools*. London: DES.

DES (1989) *Aspects of Primary Education: The Teaching and Learning of History and Geography*. London: HMSO.

DES (1992a) *Curriculum Organisation and Classroom Practice in Primary Schools: A Discussion Paper*. London: HMSO.

DES (1992b) *Starting Out with the National Curriculum*. York: NCC.

DFE (1995a) Letter from Secretary of State for Education to Schools to Introduce Revised National Curriculum.

DFE (1995b) *Key Stages 1 and 2 of the National Curriculum*. London: DFE.

Harlen, W. (1982) 'Matching', in C. Richards (ed.), *New Directions in Primary Education*. Lewes: Falmer.

HMI (1989) *Standards in Education 1987: The Annual Report of the Senior Chief Inspector Based on the Work of HMI in England*. London: DES.

HMI (1990) *Standards in Education 1988–9: The Annual Report of the Senior Chief Inspector of Schools*. London: HMSO.

NCC (1989) *A Curriculum for All: Special Needs in the National Curriculum*. York: NCC.

NCC (1992) *Starting Out with the National Curriculum*. York: NCC.

NCC/SEAC (1993a) *The National Curriculum and Its Assessment: An Interim Report by Sir Ron Dearing*. London: HMSO.

NCC/SEAC (1993b) *The National Curriculum and Its Assessment: Final Report*. London: HMSO.

NCET (1995) *Approaches to IT Capability*. Coventry: NCET.

OFSTED (1994) *Primary Matters. A Discussion on Teaching and Learning in Primary Schools.* London: HMSO.

OFSTED (1995) *The Annual Report of Her Majesty's Chief Inspector of Schools.* London: HMSO.

Papert, S. (1980) *Mindstorms: Children, Computers and Powerful Ideas.* Hemel Hempstead: Harvester Press.

Research Machines (1992) *First Word for Windows.* Oxford: Research Machines.

School Curriculum and Assessment Authority (1995) *Information Technology: The New Requirements.* London: SCAA.

Smart, L. (1992) 'Databases, history and young historians', in J. Lodge (ed.), *Computer Datahandling in the Primary School.* London: Fulton.

Smart, L. (1995) 'Facilitate and enhance', in A. Martin, L. Smart and D. Yeomans (eds), *Information Technology and the Teaching of History: International Perspectives.* Reading: Gordon and Breach.

Vygotsky, L.S. (1978) *Mind in Society: The Development of Higher Psychological Processes.* London: Harvard University Press.

Watson, D. (1993) *The ImpacT Report: An Evaluation of the ImpacT of Information Technology on Children's Achievements.* London: King's College.

Weston, P. (1992) A decade of differentiation. *British Journal of Special Education,* **19**(1), 23–31.

Index

Index